Sailboarding

Other Boating Books by A. H. Drummond, Jr.

THE COMPLETE BEGINNER'S GUIDE TO SAILING
THE COMPLETE BEGINNER'S GUIDE TO OUTBOARDING

Sailboarding

A Beginner's Guide to Boardboat Sailing

A. H. DRUMMOND, JR.

ILLUSTRATED BY SEAN MORRISON

GARDEN CITY, NEW YORK

DOUBLEDAY & COMPANY, INC.

1974

ISBN: 0-385-00453-2 Trade
0-385-08670-9 Prebound
Library of Congress Catalog Card Number 73–83627
Copyright © 1974 by A. H. Drummond, Jr.
Printed in the United States of America
First Edition

Contents

6   *Contents*

Sailboarding

With the joy of sailing clearly showing on their faces, these skippers jockey for position as they approach a mark in a closely contested race. (Photo courtesy of AMF Alcort)

1. What Is a Sailboard?

THE FIRST SAILBOARD was a surfboard with a sail tacked on. From this simple idea the sport of sailboarding has grown to be one of today's most popular forms of sailing. Sailboard hulls,* however, have been developed far beyond the surfboard stage. Today they are available in a variety of sizes, and with or without a foot well or small cockpit. Indeed, as the sailboard idea has grown in popularity, hull design has also grown, so that today some boats called sailboards might just as well be called sailboats.

* See the Glossary for the definition of all nautical terms.

The surfboarder catches a wave and uses its energy to surf along. The sailboarder does just about the same thing, except that he uses a sail to capture the energy of the wind (and stays away from the surf, unless he doesn't mind being dunked). Thus, sailboarding is surfing using wind power.

This simple idea occurred to two young men shortly after the end of World War II. They fashioned a sail and mounted it on a surfboard. They then added a rudder and tiller to steer the board, and finally, a flat centerboard or daggerboard to prevent it from slipping sideways in the water. The result, after some further refinement, was the first true sailboard: the Sailfish. This was the beginning. The end is nowhere in sight, as thousands of people, young and old, discover the thrills of sailboarding every new sailing season.

Why a sailboard? There are many reasons. Consider just a few. To begin with, sailboards are simplicity itself. There are only a few parts, and these are very easy to assemble and maintain. The boats are easily transported—two men can carry the average sailboard. Moreover, they can be trailed behind a car or even cartopped. Finally, because of their light weight and compact size, they store easily and economically during the off season.

Even more important, the sailboard is a boat for the entire family. All hands can take a turn skippering the boat. Men and women totally unfamiliar with sailing have learned quickly and easily on sailboards. Even youngsters under ten years of age have mastered the basics in short order. This simplicity is easy to understand. On most sailboards the skipper must manage just two things, the tiller and a single sail.

Where are sailboards in use? Just look around you. In general, any body of water three feet or more in

The Sailfish—the first sailboard introduced. (Photo courtesy of AMF Alcort)

One advantage of lightweight sailboard hulls is that they are easily transported—even atop compact cars. (Photo courtesy of AMF Alcort)

depth is suitable. This includes rivers, ponds, lakes, bays, harbors, even reasonably well-protected ocean areas. Getting on the water is easy. Just launch the boat from a ramp or floating dock, or drop it in and push off from shore.

Part of the fun of sailboarding is that it is often wet going. There is usually plenty of spray, especially when the breeze is up. In addition, very few sailboarders have escaped an occasional dunking. The occasional knockdown, however, just adds to the fun of sailing a sailboard. It is a simple matter to right the boat and get under way again.

It makes sense when sailboarding to be prepared for the weather and the sailing action. Wear a bathing suit or padded sailing shorts, and sneakers if the launching area is rocky. A light shirt will help ward off sunburn. In addition, and very important, the U. S. Coast Guard requires that there be an approved P.F.D.—personal flotation device (life jacket)—on board for every person on the boat. A child should always wear a life jacket when on a sailboard. For experienced swimmers, this may not be necessary, although loose life jackets are difficult to store on a sailboard. The wisest measure is to purchase the trim and lightweight sailing life jackets now widely available and insist that they be worn by everyone who sails your boat.

SAILBOARD HULLS

There are basically just two types of sailboat hulls: *displacement* hulls and *planing* hulls. Displacement hulls literally push the water aside when they are under way. The water pushed aside then fills in behind the boat as it passes. In a very real way, a displacement hull is a captive of the hole it makes in the water. Thus, the maximum speed a displacement hull can attain is limited by its shape and the amount of hull beneath the water.

Planing hulls, on the other hand, are very nearly flat-bottomed. In fact, the ideal planing hull would have a perfectly flat bottom. But such a hull would be difficult to control. In practice, planing sailboat hulls are designed in the form of a very shallow V shape that flattens out toward the stern. Sailboard hulls are constructed in this manner. In light winds and at low speeds, such hulls be-

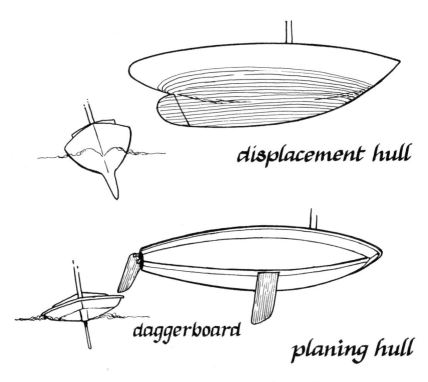

displacement hull

daggerboard

planing hull

Displacement hulls plow through the water when under way. Planing hulls, however, are designed to skim over the surface when up on plane.

have as displacement hulls—they push the water aside as they move forward. If there is enough wind and the boat is sailing flat in the water, however, this type of hull will rise out of the cavity it forms in the water and skim along the surface. This is called *planing*. Planing hulls are capable of speeds up to three times as great as those attainable by displacement hulls. One of the greatest thrills of sailboarding is getting the boat up on plane. This is often not easy to do, but it is well worth the effort.

Scow hulls are broad and flat with a blunt bow. They plane readily in moderate winds. These Butterfly class scows carry a Marconi cat rig. (Photo courtesy of Barnett Boat Company, Inc.)

A word about hull construction is in order at this point. By far the majority of commercially supplied sailboard hulls are constructed of molded Fiberglas. This material is light in weight, highly durable, has great resistence to damage, and is easy to maintain. Since sailboard hulls are really little more than hollow, airtight shells, you may someday want to build one yourself. Kits are available using molded Fiberglas or wood parts, or you can build your hull entirely of wood working from a set of plans. But more about building your own boat later.

Because of the many similarities in design and sailing characteristics, much of what we say in this book applies to *scows* as well as to sailboards. The scow type of hull was designed primarily for use on inland waters, such as lakes. These hulls are broad and flat, with a blunted bow. When heeled over sailing to windward, the broad and flat but shallow hull knifes through the water. When sailing off the wind on an even keel, however, the wide hull provides a very large planing surface. Scow hulls plane easily in moderate winds, greatly increasing their excitement potential. Scow classes range in length from about twelve feet to almost forty feet. They are raced widely throughout the country.

THE RIGS AVAILABLE

If you are new to sailing (and we assume that this is the case), then you are no doubt confused about the many different types of sail plans available. Fortunately, this problem is greatly simplified by your decision to get started with a sailboard. For while there are several different types of sailboard rigs available, there are nowhere near as many variations as on other boats.

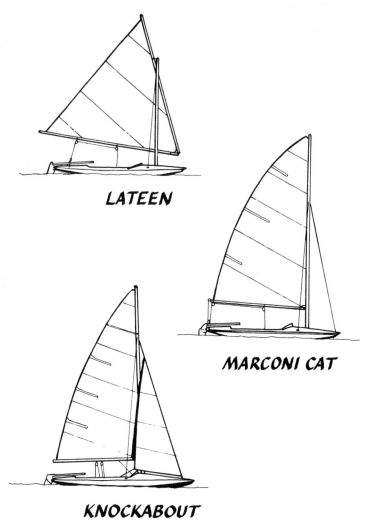

LATEEN

MARCONI CAT

KNOCKABOUT

The sail plans for the lateen, Marconi cat, and knockabout rigs.

Most sailboards carry a *lateen* rig. This rig consists of a triangular sail with the boom and gaff meeting at the forward point of the triangle. The sail is hoisted obliquely on the rather short mast. Less common, but still seen frequently, is the *Marconi cat* rig. As the term suggests, this is a cat boat rig using a Marconi sail rather than a gaff-headed sail. On such rigs, the mast is stepped well forward on the hull. The sail is triangular, and very tall along the *luff*, the forward part of the sail. The *foot*

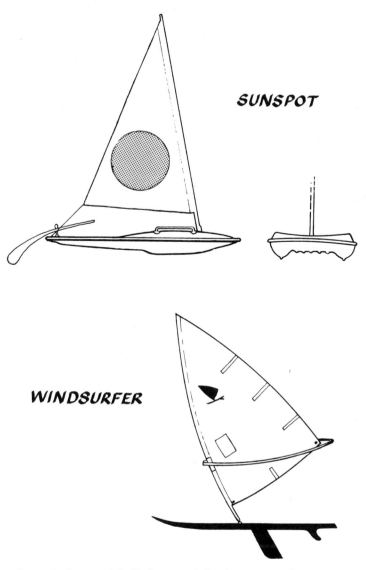

SUNSPOT

WINDSURFER

*The sail plans and hull shapes of the Sunspot and
Windsurfer.*

of the sail is short, however, compared to its height.
There is no *headsail* or *jib* (a sail rigged forward of the
mast).

Some larger sailboards and many scows are *knockabout,*
or *sloop* rigged. On this type of rig the mast is stepped
far enough aft of the bow to allow for a jib. The sail

Sunspots under way. Note the loose-footed sail and the raked mast. (Photo courtesy of Sunspot Plastics, Inc.)

plan thus consists of a Marconi mainsail and a jib. There are two advantages to this type of rig. First, there is more sail area to catch the wind. And second, when sailing to windward, the effect of the jib when it is properly set is to increase the driving efficiency of the mainsail.

Two rather unique sailboard-type boats bear special mention. The first is the Sunspot. Note that the rig used on this boat is a Marconi cat rig, but that the mast is raked back rather sharply. Note also that the sail is *loose-footed* (there is no *boom*). The most unusual characteristic of the Sunspot, however, is the absence of a centerboard or daggerboard. The manufacturer claims that the twin-keel design of the hull permits sailing without a centerboard, and also provides great stability. This boat would be worth considering if the water available for sailing were generally shallower than the three feet or so required for most sailboards.

Even more unique is the Windsurfer. Introduced just a few years ago, this unusual craft truly combines the thrills of surfing and the skills of sailing. The board is a true surfboard, and has a daggerboard but no rudder. The sail is pivoted on the deck of the board. It is controlled and trimmed by the skipper, who stands on the windward side of the sail and holds it in position by grasping the specially designed wishbone boom. Leaning

A Windsurfer beating to windward. The skipper balances the board by leaning his weight out against the force of the wind. He steers by tipping the mast either forward or aft. (Photo courtesy of Windsurfing International, Inc.)

out against the force of the wind, the skipper steers the board by raking the mast fore and aft. He turns the boat away from the wind by tipping the mast forward, and into the wind by raking it aft. The Windsurfer is said to be highly maneuverable, and just has to be the most exciting form of sailboarding available, although it does require a considerable amount of skill and strength to be sailed properly.

SAILBOARD TERMINOLOGY

Before we move on to the more technical aspects of sailing a sailboard, it is necessary to introduce some nautical terminology. The figure on page 21 shows both a lateen-rigged and a knockabout-rigged sailboard. These diagrams are labeled to show the differences between the two rigs. In addition, many terms common to all boats are shown. Mastery of nautical terminology is important, if only because sailors use it extensively, and you could be embarrassed (or perhaps injured) by not understanding something that is taking place. In addition, nautical terminology is efficient and economical of time in use. If there is an emergency when you are crewing, for example, the skipper will want quick action. He will get it if he commands, "Let go the mainsheet!" and you understand what he wants. If he must explain, however, as follows, there may not be time to avert an accident. "Do you see the large sail in back of the mast? O.K. Now, there is a rope attached to the pole at the bottom of this sail. It runs through some pulleys, and then into the cockpit, where the loose end is fastened to a cleat. Found it? Good. Untie the rope from the cleat and let the sail fly free."

This sounds ridiculous, doesn't it? And yet, it is the

LATEEN RIG

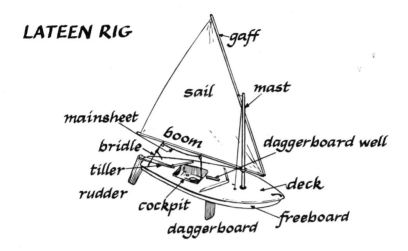

gaff

sail

mast

mainsheet

bridle

boom

daggerboard well

tiller

rudder

deck

cockpit

freeboard

daggerboard

KNOCKABOUT RIG

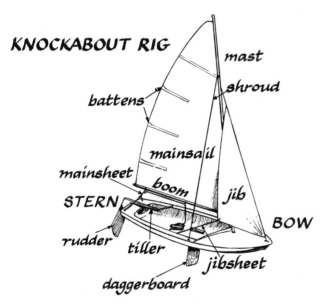

mast

shroud

battens

mainsail

mainsheet

boom

jib

STERN

rudder

tiller

BOW

jibsheet

daggerboard

Nautical terms for the principal parts of a lateen-rigged
sailboard and a knockabout-rigged sailboard. The
halyards, *the lines that raise the sails, are not shown in
these drawings.*

way we must speak on a sailboat if nautical terms are not used. Sailing, like other specialized activities, has its own vocabulary, it's own language. To be a good sailor, one must learn and then use nautical terminology. The first step is to master the terms set out in the figure. Then, whenever you are in doubt about the meaning of a term, turn to the Glossary to refresh your memory.

2. What Makes a Sailboard Go?

IF YOU ARE NEW to sailing, you probably find it surprising that fore-and-aft-rigged sailboats such as sailboards and scows can often be sailed to forty-five degrees or closer to the direction of the wind. Despite the apparent pushing effect of the wind in the opposite direction, the boat moves diagonally into the wind. It's easy, on the other hand, to see why a floating box, a cork, or a sailboat moves along with the wind behind it. In a very real way the object is being pushed along by the wind. These are the two sailing extremes; *running,* with the wind dead astern, and *beating to windward,* with the wind forty-five degrees or more ahead. In general, the same explanation applies to both extremes. Unfortunately, this explanation is a bit complicated, and involves some simple principles of aerodynamics. To grasp fully, however, why sailboards behave as they do, and to prepare yourself properly to handle a boat powered by sail, you should understand this aerodynamic explanation. With it tucked away in your mind, you will never again scratch your head in wonderment at the seemingly strange behavior of fore-and-aft-rigged sailboats.

THE SAIL AS AN AIRFOIL

While other parts of a sailboard, such as the hull, daggerboard, and rudder, no doubt help it to move, the action of the wind on the sails is the major source of driving power. It is how this drive is generated by a sail that interests us. As you may have observed, sails are cut and sewn so that they are curved, much in the same way that an airplane wing is curved. There is a good reason for this.

Let's look at how an airplane wing resembles a sail. An airplane wing is curved on top and relatively straight along the bottom. Now, when a stream of air passes over the wing, the stream divides; part goes under the wing and part goes above it. But the air going above the wing must travel a greater distance along the curve than the air streaming over the flat surface along the bottom. It turns out that the air streaming over the top moves *faster* than the air moving across the bottom of the wing. This is easy to see; since the top air must go a greater dis-

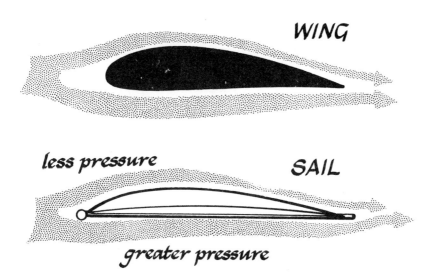

WING

less pressure   SAIL

greater pressure

*The sail is a low-speed airfoil, while the airplane wing
is a high-speed airfoil. In both cases, however, drive or
lift is generated because there is less pressure on the
convex side of the airfoil.*

tance in the same time, it must go faster. This is where
the upward force on a wing, or *lift*, comes in. As the
speed of airflow increases, the pressure it exerts decreases. Thus, the pressure of the air on top of the wing
is less than the pressure of the air on the bottom. The difference in pressure is the lift.

You can show this effect with a very simple demonstration. Take a sheet of typing paper, and blow vigor-
ously slightly down and across the top surface. The
movement of your breath across the top is much faster
than the movement of air underneath. What happens to
the paper? Do you see how the difference in pressure creates lift on the piece of paper?

Much the same thing happens on a sail when the wind
is on the beam—at right angles to the course of the boat
—or forward of the beam. As the wind strikes the sail and
divides, the difference in wind speed across the two sur-

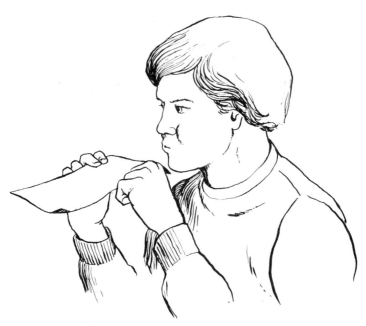

Demonstrate for yourself that pressure decreases as the speed of moving air increases. Blow slightly downward and across the top of the paper. Why does the paper rise?

faces creates a difference in pressure. This difference is the *driving force* of the sail. It occurs in the *luff*, the forward third of the sail, and is the equivalent of lift in an airplane wing. But because of the way a sail is mounted, this driving force is directed more toward the bow than toward the side of the boat.

Experiments with sails in wind tunnels show the effectiveness of this driving force on different points of sailing. When a boat is beating to windward, about 75 percent of the total drive comes from the pressure differential force. But when a boat is running with the wind dead astern, only about 25 percent of the total drive is the pressure differential force. The remaining 75 percent is the result of direct wind pressure on the sail. Thus, in a manner of speaking, a boat beating to windward is primarily pulled forward by the lift generated as the wind passes over the sails, while a boat running before the wind is primarily pushed forward by the positive pressure of the wind coming from behind the boat.

THE SLOT EFFECT

As you have probably guessed by now, the faster the wind travels over the convex side of a sail the greater the drive generated. But there is a way to get even more drive. This is where the jib of a knockabout rig comes in. The jib does two things when a boat is sailing to windward or reaching with the wind on the beam. It is an airfoil in its own right, and it generates drive. But even more important, it funnels air between itself and the convex side of the mainsail. When a stream of air is compressed into a smaller volume, as between the jib and main, the air's speed increases, although there may be turbulence.

If the jib is trimmed properly, however, its effect greatly increases the speed and smoothness of flow of the air passing between the sails. As a result, the drive generated by the mainsail is considerably increased. This is the *slot effect*. The figure on page 28 shows what happens to the airstream when the jib is eased off too far or trimmed too flat, and finally, how the airstream behaves when the jib is set just right. Clearly, this is the most important function served by the jib. Note also that the farther aft the jib extends behind the mainsail the greater the slot effect. This is the principal reason for the larger jibs, called *genoa jibs*, that you see so frequently. By extending farther aft they form a deeper slot, thus further funneling the airstream and creating even greater drive.

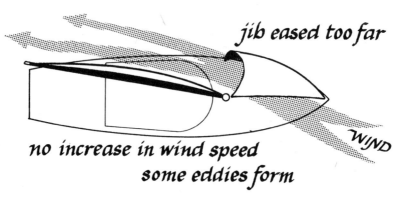

jib eased too far

no increase in wind speed
some eddies form

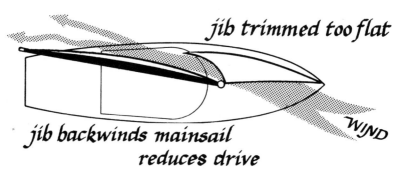

jib trimmed too flat

jib backwinds mainsail
reduces drive

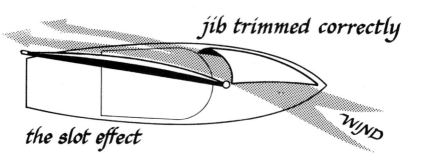

jib trimmed correctly

the slot effect

The "slot effect." When the jib is trimmed correctly,
the passage of air through the slot is speeded up. The
result is greater drive by the mainsail.

The slot effect is quite evident in this drawing of a knockabout-rigged sailboard beating to windward. Note how the shape of the jib funnels and speeds up the air as it passes between the sails. This effect greatly increases the drive of the mainsail.

WIND FORCES ON A SAILBOAT

As mentioned, the wind generates a driving force forward as it comes into contact with and passes over the sails. But with the exception of running, with the wind dead astern, a portion of the wind's energy works to make the boat heel (tip) and make leeway (move sideways in the water). Put another way, the wind does two things: It drives the boat forward, and it exerts a sideways force on the boat. Just how the wind acts to produce heeling, leeway, and forward drive is not generally well understood. To be a better sailor, however, you should know something about these effects.

Let's use a simple type of force diagram to describe how the wind's energy is divided as it strikes and passes over the sail on a lateen-rigged sailboard. To keep the explanation as simple as possible, we will avoid unneces-

Force diagram for the drive generated by the sail on a Marconi cat-rigged sailboard sailing on a beam reach.

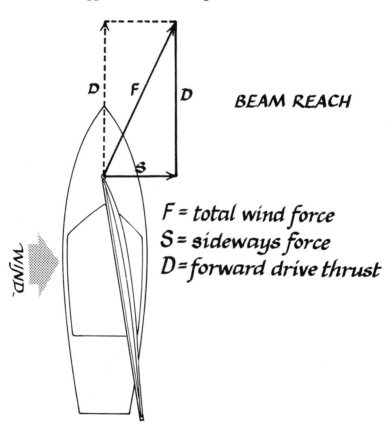

BEAM REACH

F = total wind force
S = sideways force
D = forward drive thrust

sary details, but yet include the most important aspects of the problem. To begin with, let's use arrows to represent the wind forces. As the figure on page 30 shows, these forces are: F, the total wind force; S, the sideways force that produces heel and leeway; and D, the thrust that drives the boat forward.

At this point, if you have looked at the figure carefully, you undoubtedly have a question. Why does the arrow F indicate that the total wind energy acts on the mast, if the driving force is generated in the forward third, the luff, of the sail? In somewhat simplified form, the answer is that the sail does indeed generate drive in the forward third, but it in turn acts on the mast to push the boat along. We are simplifying by assuming that all of the thrust is concentrated on the mast. Another question that may have occurred to you is this: Why are the arrows drawn with their tails to the mast, rather than the other way around? It is done this way simply for the sake of convenience. After all, does it really matter if the diagram is behind the mast and on the other side of the outline of the hull, or where we have drawn it?

Now let's look more closely at the force diagram. The boat is on a beam reach—that is, the wind is striking the sail at right angles to the course being steered. The total driving force produced by the sail is represented by the arrow F; notice its direction. This total force does two things. It drives the boat forward with that portion of the total force equal to the force D. But another portion of the total force equal to S pushes the boat sideways. The diagram is drawn as a right triangle because the two forces, S and D, acting together at right angles to each other produce the same result as the single force F.

No doubt you are now wondering what happens when the wind strikes the boat and sail at other angles. Let's

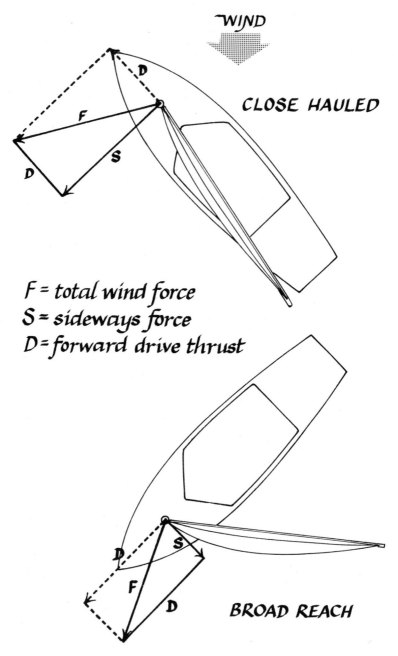

WIND

CLOSE HAULED

F = total wind force
S = sideways force
D = forward drive thrust

BROAD REACH

Force diagrams for a sailboard on a broad reach and
closehauled.

look at two additional situations: the broad reach, with the wind coming from astern, but at an angle; and beating to windward, or closehauled, with the wind approximately forty-five degrees ahead. On a broad reach, the total driving force F is directed more toward the bow of the boat. As a result, the driving force D is greater and the sideways force S is less than on a beam reach. It shouldn't surprise you to learn that a boat on a broad reach heels less and makes less leeway than a boat on a beam reach.

When the boat is closehauled, however, the total driving force is directed more toward the side of the boat. The result, in this case, is a smaller driving force D and a larger sideways force S. Now you know why sailboards that are beating to windward heel so much. You can see too why the skipper and crew hike out to offset the sideways force causing the boat to heel.

FUNCTION OF THE DAGGERBOARD, TILLER, AND RUDDER

Because the sideways force S is largest when the boat is closehauled, this is the point of sailing that will produce the greatest heeling and the greatest leeway. But the daggerboard or keel offers resistance to any sideways movement of the boat, thus reducing leeway. Heeling occurs because the boat resists sideways motion; it rotates on an axis that runs the length of the boat near the waterline. As the boat heels, however, air spills out of the sails. The boat then stops heeling when the forces on the hull tending to right it just equalize the wind pressure tending to heel the boat over.

Let's take a closer look at and also compare the forces acting on both a keel boat and a sailboard when the craft

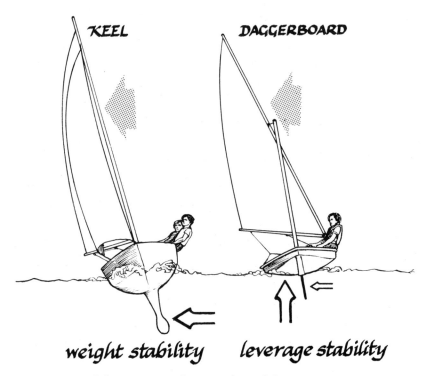

KEEL   **DAGGERBOARD**

weight stability   leverage stability

Leverage stability compared to weight stability. In leverage stability, the buoyant effect on the side of the hull away from the wind is the most important factor. In weight stability, the weight of the keel is the most important factor.

are heeled over. On the keel boat, the principal force off-setting the heeling effect of the wind is *weight stability*. This, as you can see, is the result of a very heavy keel being placed low in the water beneath the hull of the boat.

The daggerboard of a sailboard, however, is usually very light in weight. Thus a daggerboard contributes only a small amount of weight stability. Additional stability is therefore required on a sailboard. This is contributed in the form of buoyancy, as shown in the figure. Sailboard hulls are shaped in such a way that buoyant force acts to right them when they are heeled over. This is called *leverage stability*. This effect is not produced on the round bottom of a typical keel boat.

On a sailboard, the skipper often has both hands fully occupied. In one hand he controls the sheet, the line that sets the position of the sail (although the crew sometimes handles the sheet), and with the other he operates the tiller. The tiller is a handle fitted to the head of the rudder post. It extends forward from the stern, placing it in a convenient position for handling.

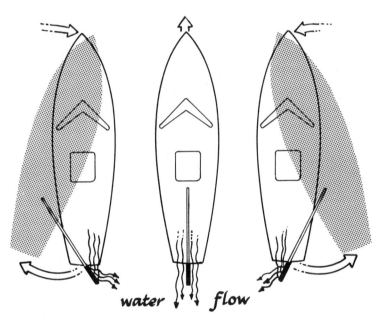

water flow

Water forces on the rudder of a sailboard, and how these forces make the hull turn. Note that in a turn the stern shifts to the side to point the bow of the boat in the new direction.

Moving the tiller moves the rudder, and thus controls the direction of sailing. As the figure on this page shows, when the tiller is moved to port (left, facing forward), the stern moves to port and the bow turns to starboard (right, facing forward). Conversely, when the tiller is moved to starboard, the stern moves to starboard and the bow turns to port. When the tiller and rudder are in line with the keel, of course, there is no turning effect.

It is sometimes hard for beginners to grasp just how a boat turns. Many believe that boats turn the same way autos do—that is, the front end turns and the rear end follows the path the front end describes. This is not the case at all with boats. On a car, the steering is accomplished by wheels that turn at the front. On a boat, the rudder is mounted at the stern. Thus one literally points the front of a car in the direction desired, while on a boat the position of the stern is shifted until the bow points in the desired direction. Many an inexperienced sailor has been embarrassed by ramming neighboring boats or a dock with a swinging stern.

Look at the figure again. It shows how inserting the rudder into the smooth stream of water passing under the boat makes the boat change course. As the rudder is turned, it interferes with the passage of flowing water. The water thus exerts pressure on the side of the rudder facing forward. This pressure causes the stern to swing in the direction the tiller is pointing. Of course, when the rudder is in line with the daggerboard or keel, the water pressure on both sides is the same, and no turning effect occurs.

There are two additional points worth noting. First, because a turned rudder interferes with the flow of water around the hull, it has a braking effect on the speed of the boat. Second, there is a rudder angle for every boat that produces the greatest turning effect. If the rudder is turned to a greater angle, its effect is to slow the boat down more than to turn it. In the extreme, if the rudder is turned a full ninety degrees, it does little or no turning and acts mostly as a brake.

As you have probably noticed, for the rudder to exert a turning effect, water must be flowing around it. But, of course, for water to stream by the rudder, the boat must be under way—that is, it must be moving. In nautical terms, *steerage way* is the slowest speed at which a boat can be steered. At lower speeds the boat simply does not respond to the helm; in a sense, it is nearly dead in the water.

Sailboards should be easy to steer. Indeed, if a boat is well balanced, the tiller is quite light to the touch. One hand is usually sufficient; sometimes it is even possible to handle the tiller with just the fingertips. It is important to remember that rudder shifts should be smooth and gentle, with the smallest possible movement. Sharply yanking the tiller back and forth slows a boat, for as pointed out, a turned rudder exerts a braking effect.

3. Wind, Water, and Sail

IN THE CHAPTER just completed, when we explained how the wind drives a sailboard, we used such terms as *beating, reaching,* and *running.* These terms describe the basic sailing positions relative to the wind. Up to this point it was enough for you to have just a general idea of what they mean. Now it becomes necessary to look more closely at their meanings, for it is important when actually sailing to have a firm understanding of how the wind and a boat interact.

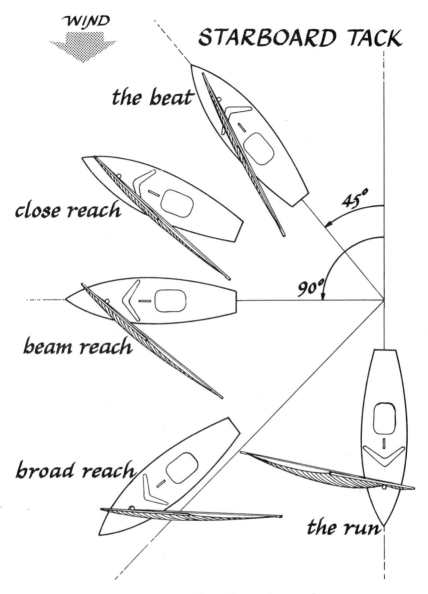

the beat

close reach

45°

90°

beam reach

broad reach

the run

The basic sailing positions, and how they relate to the
direction of the wind. If conditions are right, it is possible
to get a sailboard on a beam reach to plane.

The figure on this page shows the positions of a sailboard and the sail settings relative to the wind for all
courses on the *starboard tack*. When a boat is on the star-

board tack, the wind is coming in over the starboard side of the boat. For the *port tack*—wind coming in over the port side of the boat—just picture the mirror image of the diagram. All of the positions for the port tack are exactly opposite those shown.

Sailboats are sailed either *to windward* or *to leeward*. Whenever the bow of the boat is more into the wind than away from the wind, it is sailing to windward. Beating and close reaching are windward courses. The dividing line is the beam reach; when a boat is on a beam reach, the wind is at right angles to the course of the boat. Finally, when the bow of the boat is away from the wind, the boat is sailing to leeward. Broad reaching and running are leeward courses.

Let's look more closely at beating, reaching, and running to acquire a feeling for how the boat behaves and what it is like to be on board on these basic sailing positions.

BEATING

When a sailboard is beating, it is sailing as close to the wind as possible—but usually not closer than forty-five degrees to the wind direction. Sailing closehauled requires careful attention to several details. The boom is trimmed down-and-out to the lee quarter in order to flatten the mainsail. The jib, if you are sailing a knockabout-rigged sailboard, is sheeted in carefully to produce the best possible slot effect. This is the position of sailing with the greatest sideways effect of the wind's energy, hence it is often necessary to climb up and out on the windward side of the boat to counteract heeling. This is called "hiking out." Several of the photos in the book show you that hiking out can sometimes be quite an acrobatic stunt.

These Butterfly class scows are beating to windward.
Note how the boom is trimmed down and out to the lee
quarter. (Photo courtesy of Barnett Boat Company, Inc.)

In order to find the course for beating—that is, to get
as close to the wind as possible without luffing—follow
these steps. Sheet in the mainsail (and jib on a knockabout-rigged boat) and slowly head up into the wind
until the mainsail luffs (flaps, or backwinds). Then ease
off until the luffing stops. This is your course. The sail(s)
should be full and drawing well. If you are holding
course, but the sail begins to luff, it means the wind has
shifted ahead—that is, it has *hauled*. Fall off until the

luffing stops. If you suspect that the wind has shifted more toward the stern—that is, has *veered*—head up into the wind until the sail begins to luff. Easing off until the luffing stops then gives you the new course.

When beating, it is important to check the condition of the boat constantly. For example, if you seem to be going too slowly, fall off a bit. It's possible to point too close to the wind; this costs speed. You might try easing the sheets a bit also, because pinching the sail(s) will slow a boat. Always keep an eye on the forward third of the mainsail. This is where luffing first occurs; it therefore tells you wind direction at once.

REACHING

In general, there are three reaching positions: the *close reach,* the *beam reach,* and the *broad reach.* All lie between beating and running before the wind. In many respects, reaching gives the sailor the most fun for his efforts. The boat usually heels less on a reach than when beating, and goes faster because a greater portion of the total wind force goes into drive. In addition, the boat is usually in better balance on a reach. As a result, handling is easier.

The close reach lies between the beat and the beam reach. To set the sail for a close reach, first put the boat on course. Then ease out the sheet until the sail begins to luff. At this point, haul in the sheet until the fluttering stops. Perform the same procedure with both the mainsail and jib if your sailboard is knockabout rigged. If you have been careful, this should involve hauling in only a few inches of sheet line.

On a beam reach the wind is ninety degrees to the course of the boat, or close to it. To set the sails for a beam reach, follow the procedure outlined above for the close reach. On many boats, this is the most exciting point of sailing. It is very fast, and if the rig is tuned properly, quite thrilling. With a bit of skill and luck, or a combination of both, you may even get your sailboard to plane. You haven't really experienced the thrills of sailing until you get a boat up on a plane. But more about planing a bit later.

This Bonito class boat is on a beam reach. On this point of sailing the wind strikes the boat at approximately ninety degrees to the course being steered. (Photo courtesy of Lincoln Fiberglass, Inc.)

Your boat is on a broad reach when the wind is coming from aft of the beam but not directly astern. Once again, the technique in setting the sails is to put the boat on course, ease out the sheet line until the sail begins to luff, and then haul in the sheet until the luffing stops. If your boat has a masthead wind pennant, a good rule of thumb is to set the boom at an angle halfway between the line of the keel and the direction the wind pennant is pointing.

In a good breeze, with moderate seas running, a boat on a broad reach will surf down the front of waves as they pass under the boat. This is indeed exciting sailing.

RUNNING

A sailboat is running before the wind when the wind comes from astern or slightly on the quarter. To set the sail, the sheet line is eased out until the boom is nearly at right angles to the centerline of the boat. If a boom vang is available, this is one time to use it, for the main should be as flat as possible. Without a vang, the boom will ride up and the mainsail will billow. This alters the sail's shape and results in decreased drive. The vang also serves to prevent an accidental jibe.

The jib on a knockabout rig is useless on a run because it is blanketed by the mainsail. It is possible, however, to hold the jib out on the side opposite the main by a pole. The pole—called a whisker pole—extends from the clew of the jib to a point somewhere on the mast. A boat sailing this way is said to be sailing *wing-and-wing*.

As picturesque as sailing wing-and-wing is, it is not particularly fast, especially in very light winds. Clearly, since the principal driving force when running is the direct pressure of the wind on the sails, to increase speed it is necessary to increase sail area. This is accomplished on

*When the wind is dead astern, or very nearly so, the
boat is said to be running before the wind. The boom
and sail on this Aeronaut class boat are set correctly,
with the boom at about ninety degrees to the centerline
of the hull. (Photo by Stanley Rosenfeld, courtesy of
Aero-Nautical, Inc.)*

many boats by flying a spinnaker. The spinnaker mark-
edly increases the speed of a boat when running or broad
reaching, for it offers much more sail area to the wind
than a jib. The use of a spinnaker on a sailboard, however, is not practical.

PLANING

Because of the way they are constructed, sailboard hulls will plane under the right conditions. Of course, it takes some skillful sailing on the part of the skipper to get a sailboard up on a plane. The effort, however, is worth all the trouble. It will help in mastering this skill to understand what happens when a boat goes up on a plane.

All boats make a bow wave and stern wave as they move through the water. In a very real way, the boat's

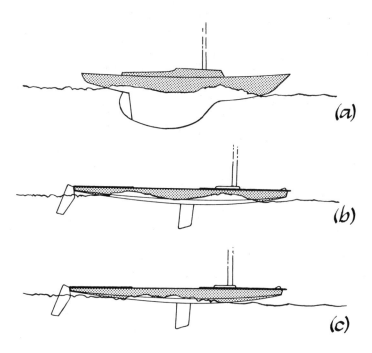

(a)

(b)

(c)

(a) A displacement hull forming a bow wave and a stern wave. (b) At low speeds sailboard hulls act as displacement hulls. (c) When on a plane, a sailboard hull skims along on top of its own bow wave.

hull sits in a trough surrounded in part, at least, by the bow wave and the stern wave. This trough acts as a trap for displacement hulls (and also for planing hulls when not on a plane; see the figure on page 46). After a certain speed—the so-called hull speed—is reached, it is not possible for a sailboat hull to go any faster. To go faster, it would have to climb out of the trough and up the bow wave. Displacement hulls, however, can't do this because of their shape and weight.

Planing hulls, on the other hand, are designed to escape the wave trap. Such hulls differ from displacement hulls in that they are light in weight and very nearly flat-bottomed. With sufficient wind, they can be forced out of the trough and up onto the bow wave. Once up on the bow wave, the boat's flat bottom produces lift and keeps the boat on the surface. As long as it remains on a plane, the hull will skim over the surface at speeds much greater than displacement speeds.

Several conditions must be met to get a sailboard up on a plane. First, the boat must be sailed flat. This means that you will have to hike out to counterbalance the heeling effect of the wind. Second, the boat must be on a beam reach, or very nearly a beam reach. And third, the wind must be brisk—perhaps ten knots or more.

If these conditions are met—with experience, you will learn to sense when a boat is nearing planing conditions —quick and decisive action is needed to get it up on the plane. Hike out to keep the hull flat in the water. Bounce forward when the boat is on the front of a wave and then back as the wave passes to keep the bow up out of the water. Some sailboarders call this *ooching*. Pump the sail —that is, trim it in sharply to lift the bow out of the water —and rock, which helps also to lift the bow.

Once on a plane, keep the hull flat and parallel to the water. Stay near the middle of the boat, for if the bow comes up, the stern will squat deeper and build up drag. As mentioned, getting a sailboard to plane is not easy, although it clearly offers the most sailing fun there is to be had. Try it, and don't be discouraged. It takes practice. Be prepared too to get wet. It's a sure bet that you'll take an occasional dunking learning to get your sailboard up on a plane.

WIND AND A MOVING BOAT

Earlier in this chapter we mentioned *hauling* and *veering*. The wind is said to haul when it changes direction toward the bow of the boat. It is said to veer when it changes direction toward the stern. Both of these changes are in relation to the boat—that is, we are looking at wind change from the point of view of the boat.

It is also possible to view change in wind direction from the point of view of the horizon. Suppose the wind is coming from the north—we call this a north wind (wind is always named by the compass point from which it comes). Now, when the wind changes in an easterly direction (clockwise), it is said to *veer*. On the other hand, when it swings to westward (counterclockwise), it is said to *back*.

Additional new terminology is needed to describe how the wind comes in to a moving boat. It may, for example, strike the boat anywhere from dead ahead all the way to dead astern, either on the starboard or port side. The figure gives these new terms. They are exactly the same on the opposite side of the boat.

When the wind is coming from within 45 degrees of the heading of the boat, it is referred to as *wind ahead*.

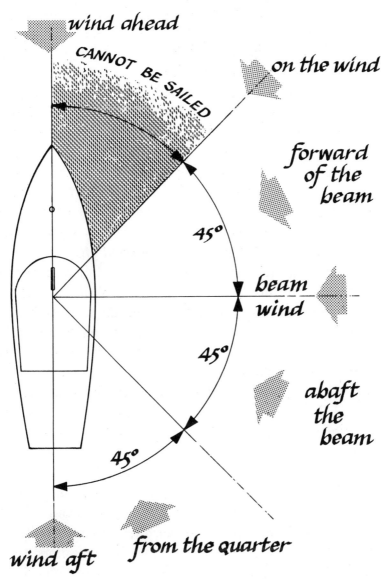

wind ahead

CANNOT BE SAILED

on the wind

forward
of the
beam

45°

beam
wind

45°

abaft
the
beam

45°

from the quarter

wind aft

Terminology for wind direction as it relates to a boat
under sail.

The 45-degree angle may vary. As we have pointed out, most boats will point up to about 45 degrees, while many others do not even reach the 45-degree mark. When the wind is from the direction at which the boat points most efficiently, the term is *on the wind*.

Between the beating angle and almost directly abeam, the wind is *forward of the beam*. Then, when the wind is directly on the beam—a point 90 degrees from the heading of the boat—it is a *beam wind*. Wind arriving from a direction between 90 and 135 degrees from the bow is *wind abaft the beam*. *Wind from the quarter* is then wind coming in from 135 to 180 degrees from the heading of the boat. Finally, wind coming from directly behind the boat is called *wind astern* or *wind aft*.

Pennants and *telltales*—pieces of cloth ribbon or yarn—attached to the masthead or shrouds indicate the direction of the wind on a boat. It's important to understand, however, that on a moving boat the pennants and telltales do not tell you the *true direction* of the wind. They tell you the direction of the *apparent wind*. Here's why. With the true wind on the beam, and the boat sailing forward, the pennant drags behind a bit because it is affected by the air the boat is moving through as well as by the beam wind. The result on the wind pennant is an angle slightly aft of the angle that would have been produced if the boat were standing still. Thus, the position of the pennant on a moving boat makes the wind appear to be coming from a point farther ahead than it really is. This is the *apparent wind* direction. Many sailors refer frequently to the telltale while sailing because its position is an indication of the direction of the wind relative to the heading of the boat. As the diagram suggests, the telltale angle can help the skipper hold his course when the wind is constant, and it quickly reveals a wind shift when the wind is variable. A wind shift, of course, should be followed by an adjustment of the sail settings. The beginning sailor in particular will find keeping a close watch on the telltale a good habit to cultivate.

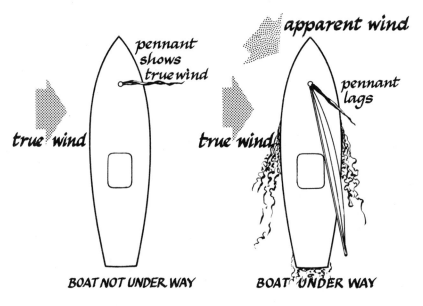

The apparent wind direction is slightly forward of the true wind direction. Apparent wind occurs because the pennant is affected by the air the boat is moving through as well as by the wind.

4. Under Way!

IT'S ONE THING to *understand* what is happening on board a boat that is under way, and quite another to *experience* these events. There is no substitute for actually sailing your own sailboard, as you will discover when you first try it yourself. In the meantime, we will attempt to describe what is involved in a short sail. We'll start with launching the boat from the beach. Then, after putting the craft through its paces on open water, we'll return to the beach. Later we will discuss the rules that govern the

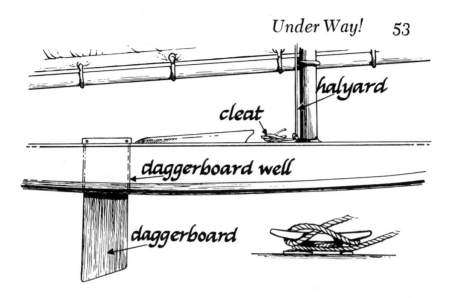

How the halyard is fastened to a cleat on the deck of a typical sailboard.

movements of boats in channels and anchorages, and under heavy traffic conditions.

Before getting under way, it is necessary to describe the rigging that controls the sails. These lines are known collectively as the *running rigging.* On a typical sailboard, such as the lateen-rigged Sunfish, the running rigging consists of just two lines: the *halyard,* used to raise the sail on the mast, and the *sheet line,* used to trim the sail in when the boat is under way. If your sailboard is knockabout rigged, there will be a halyard and a sheet line for the jib also. Each halyard, of course, passes through a pulley or an eye at the top of the mast and is secured to a cleat at the bottom of the mast or on the deck. The sheet line for the sail is attached through a bridle to the deck near the stern and then passes through one or more pulleys on the boom before leading into the cockpit.

*How the sheet line is fastened to the bridle at the stern
of the boat. The tape on the tiller protects it from chafing.*

LAUNCHING FROM THE BEACH

Since by far the majority of sailboards in use are lateen rigged, we'll describe in detail how to launch this type of boat. If your boat is cat or knockabout rigged, the principles involved will be the same, although the actual procedures will differ somewhat. Getting ready to launch is simplicity itself. With the boat on the beach or on a launching dolly (or floating in shallow water), prepare the sail and spars and other gear as follows: First, lash the sail to the spars and secure the halyard to the upper spar, as directed by the rigging instructions that come

All running rigging and gear ready for launching. The sails are left out of this drawing in order to show the different parts more clearly.

with the boat. The other end of the halyard is then run through the pulley at the top of the mast. Refer again to the instructions, and run the sheet line through the pulleys on the lower spar; fasten the end of the sheet line to the bridle at the stern of the boat. Next, run the bottom end of the mast through the ring on the lower spar and drop the mast into the mast hole on the deck of the boat. The sail is now rigged and ready to be raised, although it is still necessary to rig the rudder and daggerboard and then launch the boat.

To launch, first make sure the rain plug (if there is one) is screwed in place, and then shove the boat into shallow water. Attach the rudder to the stern of the boat, and place the daggerboard in the cockpit or on the deck. You are now ready to launch, but note again that the law now requires that a Coast Guard-approved life preserver be on board for every person on the boat.

To get under way, first walk the boat out to waist-deep water, then drop the daggerboard into the well and shove it all the way down. Now aim the bow of the boat its cleat while continuing to hold the bow of the boat into the wind and raise the sail. Secure the halyard to into the wind. The sail should flap loosely (*luff*) in the breeze much as a flag does. Get aboard by pushing off and then jumping onto the boat just astern of the cockpit. As you jump aboard, hold the sheet line in one hand and the tiller in the other.

Once aboard and in control, pull the tiller toward you to turn the bow away from the direction of the wind. This will result in the wind coming in to the boat on an angle. Sheet in the sail until it fills and the boat begins to make headway. If this maneuver is done efficiently, you should be sailing either closehauled or on a close reach.

*The breeze is up, and these young sailors are getting
ready to launch. (Photo by Dorothy I. Crossley)*

So far, so good! You're under way and headed for open
water. But what do you do when you want the boat to go
in another direction? This is a good question, for regard-
less of whether you are sailing simply for the pleasure of
it, with no particular destination in mind, or you are sailing to a particular point, it is necessary to know how to
sail a boat in all directions. As indicated earlier, you
can't always point the boat in the desired direction and
sail away. For example, you already know that it is impossible to sail directly into the wind. How then does the
sailor take his boat to a destination that lies directly upwind?

To take a boat to a point directly upwind, it is necessary to sail a zigzag course. This is called *tacking*. Each
leg of the zigzag course is sailed as closehauled as possible, with an angle of about ninety degrees between
courses. As the figure shows, this ninety-degree angle between tacks results because the boat sails closehauled at
about forty-five degrees to the wind.

There are two ways to tack to a point directly upwind.
Frequent short tacks or fewer long tacks may be made.
The choice between short and long tacks is a matter of
judgment. You will have to evaluate each situation you
find yourself in and then act accordingly. Experience
helps a great deal, as you will discover when you have
been sailing for a while. We might make one suggestion,
however. Try not to lose sight of your point or marker—
that is, the place you are trying to reach. This marker
may be a buoy, a flagpole, or a house of a particular color
or shape on shore. By taking a series of short tacks, you
can usually keep this marker in sight. On the other hand,
if you take a long tack, you may sail out of sight of the
marker. You may even sail far above it and lose time as a
result.

Now, suppose you are on the last tack. How do you
judge when to come about so that the boat will sail directly to the marker? The answer is quite simple. If the
boat is capable of sailing at forty-five degrees to the
wind, you must wait until the mark is exactly on the
beam—that is, at ninety degrees to the course of the boat.
This is easy to judge. Face forward and extend your arm
at right angles to the course of the boat on the side of the
marker. Sight along your arm. When it points directly at
your destination, continue on course for a bit to allow for

Tacking is sailing a zigzag course upwind. One must tack in a sailboard to reach a destination that lies in the windward direction.

leeway, and then come about. Of course, if your boat does not point as close as forty-five degrees to the wind, an angle greater than ninety degrees will be necessary.

Up to this point, we have spoken of tacking without paying any attention to the technique of turning a sailboat so that the wind is changed from one side to the other. There are two ways to do this: *coming about* and *jibing*. Let's look at coming about first.

COMING ABOUT

When a sailboard comes about, it has changed from one tack to the other, with the bow swinging through the eye of the wind.

If you study the figure on page 61, you will get a clear picture of the events that take place during the coming-about maneuver. Let's assume, for example, that we are sailing closehauled on the port tack, and it is decided to come about. The helmsman gives the command, "Ready about!" This alerts the crew to be ready to handle the sheet line and move to the other side of the boat. A few moments later, after the crew is ready, the helmsman gives the command, "Hard-a-lee!" to actually begin the maneuver.

Several events then take place at the same time. First, the helmsman puts the tiller over to leeward, causing the bow to swing into the wind. The bow then swings through the eye of the wind, with the sail luffing, and falls off with the wind on the other side. The sail will then fill with the wind right away if the sheet line has been held taut. During these maneuvers, the crew, including the helmsman, has been moving across the boat to the other side. The crew members time their movements as the boat turns so that they arrive to windward just as the sail fills and the boat moves off on its new course. Finally, the tiller is put amidships, and the boat is steered to its new course.

We have described coming about with a crew member aboard handling the sheet line. If you are sailing alone, of course, you will have to handle both the tiller and the sheet line yourself. This takes practice and a bit of skill. Be sure too to keep your head down when the boom

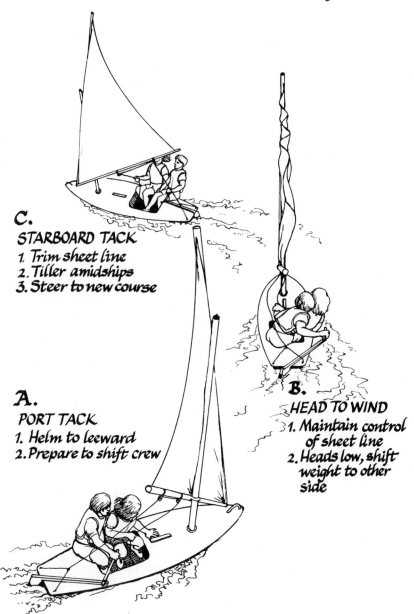

C.
STARBOARD TACK
1. Trim sheet line
2. Tiller amidships
3. Steer to new course

A.
PORT TACK
1. Helm to leeward
2. Prepare to shift crew

B.
HEAD TO WIND
1. Maintain control
   of sheet line
2. Heads low, shift
   weight to other
   side

The sequence of events that takes place when coming about. See the text for a more detailed description.

passes overhead. Many a careless sailor has taken a nasty whack on the head while coming about.

Sailboards lose a great deal of their momentum when coming about. It is important therefore to execute this maneuver sharply, for the boat may not complete the turn. If this happens, the boat will end up dead in the water, with the bow into the wind and the sail luffing. This can occur for a variety of reasons. The boat may have had insufficient way on, or the crew's weight may have been poorly distributed. As mentioned, the helmsman may not have brought the boat around smartly enough, or he may have jammed the tiller over too rapidly, causing the rudder to act as a brake. In any event, when this happens the boat is said to be *in irons*. It refuses to answer to the helm, and drifts backward helplessly. Eventually, as it drifts back, the boat will fall off one way or the other, and the sail will fill. There is no way of knowing, however, whether it will fall off on the tack the skipper wants.

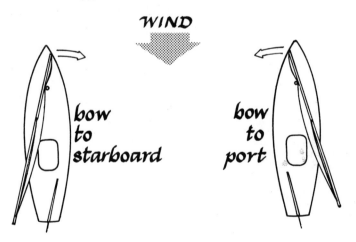

When caught "in irons," put the sail aback to turn the boat off the wind.

Of course, it is best to avoid getting into irons, but should it happen, correction is fairly simple. The trick is to put the sail aback so that the bow will fall off in the desired direction. To make the bow go to starboard and put the boat on the port tack, turn the tiller to starboard, and then grab the boom by hand and hold the sail out on the port side. Just the opposite is done to make the bow fall off to port. As the boat falls off, wait until the wind is just slightly forward of the beam before setting the tiller for the new course and trimming the sheet line.

JIBING

When a sailboat jibes, the boat is brought around to the opposite tack by putting the stern through the eye of the wind. In effect, jibing is the opposite of coming about. A boat is usually jibed when sailing before the wind and a course change is desired, but the skipper wants to avoid coming about. Sometimes when sailing downwind, the wind will shift so that it is coming from the same side of the boat the boom is on. This is called sailing *by the lee*. It is a dangerous condition, for the wind may get behind the sail and produce an accidental jibe. The rapidly swinging boom of an accidental jibe can be very dangerous to the crew and rigging.

The jibe should not be attempted in strong winds by beginning sailors. Not only is the flying boom a hazard to the crew, there is also the possibility that its momentum will damage the rigging or perhaps even dismast the boat. It is much safer to sheet in the sail, come about, and then ease off to the new course.

The jibe is easy to perform, however, in light and moderate winds. Here's how it is done. Assume the boat is on

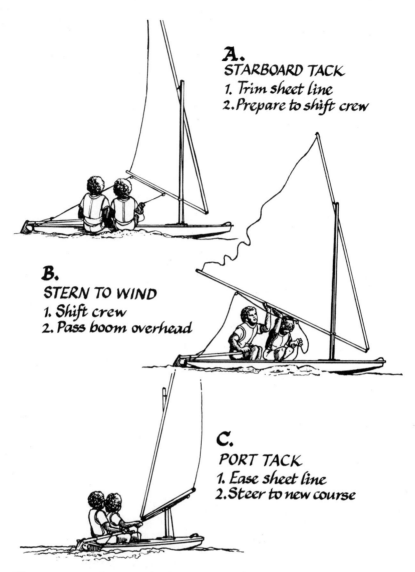

A.
STARBOARD TACK
1. Trim sheet line
2. Prepare to shift crew

B.
STERN TO WIND
1. Shift crew
2. Pass boom overhead

C.
PORT TACK
1. Ease sheet line
2. Steer to new course

*The sequence of events during "jibing." A boat should
be jibed in light-to-moderate winds only. In heavy winds
jibing is a dangerous maneuver.*

a broad reach with the boom eased well out from the
boat. Make sure the daggerboard is fully lowered to add
stability. To begin the jibe, haul in the sheet line to bring

the boom in toward the centerline of the boat. Hold course while bringing in the boom, and then change course. The boom will swing over to the other side of the boat as the wind gets behind it. Shift the crew to the other side of the boat at this time. Next, quickly ease out the sheet line until the sail is in position for the new course.

Special precautions must be followed when handling the sail during a jibe. The sheet line should never be fastened, but rather hauled and held by hand. In addition, the sheet must be kept clear so that it can be run out after jibing without snarling.

Sometimes, when a boat is sailing downwind, the wind will repeatedly shift a few degrees back and forth. This makes it difficult to sail without jibing. But if the wind is strong and the seas rough, the wise skipper won't want to jibe. The preferred tactic under these conditions is to *tack downwind.* In tacking downwind, a zigzag course downwind is followed. The boat is sailed on a broad reach. When the opposite tack is desired, the boat is brought all the way around and up into the wind; it comes about and then falls off to a broad reach. Coming about is always safer than jibing. Moreover, when tacking downwind the boat is sailing on a broad reach, which is safer than running with the wind directly astern. When the wind is directly astern, there is always the possibility of an accidental jibe.

RIGHTING A CAPSIZED SAILBOARD

Part of the fun of sailboarding is the occasional knockdown and dunking. Although experienced sailboarders will be dunked only rarely, the beginner can expect to be in the water often until he masters the art of sailing the

Righting a sailboard is easy. Simply place a foot on the daggerboard and hands on the deck side or rail. Body weight will then right the boat. (Photo courtesy of AMF Alcort)

boat. No one, however, should allow fear of capsizing to deter him from learning to sail a sailboard. With few exceptions these boats are very easy to right. And once righted, they are ready to sail again immediately.

When you find yourself in the water hanging onto a sailboard floating on its side, just follow this simple procedure to get going again. First swim the boat around so that the bow is pointing into the wind. Then, grasping the handrail or edge of the deck with both hands, simply stand up on the daggerboard so that your weight will pivot the boat into the upright position. It's so easy even a child can do it! When the boat has been righted, climb aboard, regain control of the sheet line and tiller, put the sail aback, and sail off.

Virtually all sailboards are unsinkable. Thus, if you capsize and for some reason cannot right the boat, STAY WITH IT!! Do not attempt to swim to shore. No matter how easy it may look, your chances are infinitely greater with the boat than leaving it. Far too many fatal accidents result from failure to follow this basic rule of boating: If your boat floats when swamped or capsized, stay with it; do not leave it until you are picked up by another boat or drift ashore. Remember too that the law now requires that each person on board have a life preserver. Wearing the preserver and staying with the boat, you are far safer than striking out for shore.

RETURNING TO THE BEACH

With our little demonstration sail finished, it's time to return to the beach. We've tacked upwind and downwind, mastered the arts of coming about and jibing, and learned how to right a capsized boat. Sailing a sailboard into the beach is no more difficult than launching. Simply head the boat in, pull the daggerboard out of its well just before the water becomes too shallow, and coast in. If the rudder of your boat is the tip-up type, it will pivot up when the lower edge touches bottom. If it is not the tip-up type, you will have to lift it out of its fittings before it strikes the bottom. Try to release the sheet line and let the sail go slack a few moments before the boat grounds on the beach. It is a simple task at this point to drop the sail, put everything in order, and move the boat to its place of storage.

5. Sailing and the Weather

THERE IS AN old saying that goes as follows: "The good seaman weathers the storm he cannot avoid, and he avoids the storm he cannot weather." For all sailors, but especially the small-boat sailor, it is important to learn how to "read" the weather. If there is one single factor that dominates sailing, it is the weather. Thus, the knowledgeable sailboarder is always prepared on three counts: (1) he never goes out without obtaining the latest

For Period Ending 7 AM EST 6/14/73. During Wednesday night, showers and thunderstorms will be indicated over most of the Rockies, the mid Atlantic states, the Eastern half of Texas and also in Southern Florida. Clear to partly elsewhere. Minimum readings include: (approx. maximum temperatures in parenthesis) Atlanta 66(85), Boston 56(78), Chicago 56(78), Cleveland 53(75), Dallas 69(90), Denver 50(91), Duluth 44(72), Jacksonville 71(91), Kansas City 66(87), Little Rock 68(86), Los Angeles 57(70), Miami 74(89), Minneapolis 50(86), New Orleans 70(87), New York 65(79), Phoenix 69(94), San Francisco 50(72), Seattle 46(65), St. Louis 64(85) and Washington 66(85).

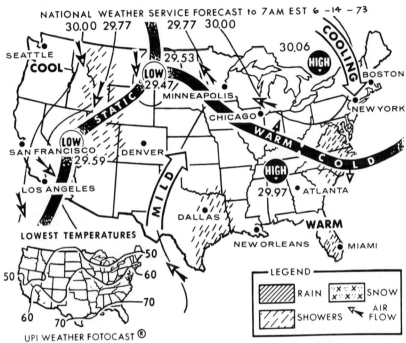

A typical newspaper weather map. Note the highs and the lows, and the isobars—lines drawn through points of equal barometric pressure. The temperature lines shown on the lower map are called isotherms.

weather report; (2) while sailing, he continually watches for indications of an adverse weather change; and (3) when such a weather change seems probable, he takes appropriate action at once. He does not wait, thinking (usually incorrectly) that the change won't occur for a while, or that he has plenty of time before the storm or squall hits.

Keeping on top of the weather is by no means as difficult as it may seem. This is particularly true of obtaining weather reports before going out, for a number of
sources are readily available. Virtually every newspaper
contains a daily weather map that gives the weather situation throughout the entire country. What is just as important, however, is that these maps allow rough-weather
predictions for up to a day or so in advance. Become
familiar with the map in your local paper. Learn the
symbols, and study the map daily for a period of weeks
or months. This will establish in your mind the normal
weather patterns for your area, and enable you to make a
reasonably good prediction on any given day. The figure
on page 69 is a typical weather map. Television weather
reports and forecasts are perhaps even better, for they
provide a more up-to-date analysis of the local situation.
Many of these programs, as you know, include a thorough weather-map analysis. If you plan to go sailing the
following day, make it a practice to watch the TV
weather report the night before. Radio forecasts are important also. You are no doubt familiar with the brief
forecasts given often during regular programming. What
you may not know is that many stations in coastal areas
broadcast periodic marine weather forecasts. These reports are quite thorough; they are essential to the careful
sailboarder. If you cannot find station listings for marine
forecasts in the paper, call your local Coast Guard station for the necessary information.

A good barometer hanging on the wall at home is very
useful also. This instrument, as you probably know, measures the pressure exerted by the atmosphere. In general,
the drier the air, the greater the pressure it exerts. A rising barometer often means clearing, with fair weather
ahead. A falling barometer, on the other hand, usually

means bad weather, with rain and cloudy conditions. Do not rely on a barometer if you have access to other, more reliable sources of weather information. A barometer allows a very rough forecast only; it should not be looked upon as an infallible instrument.

As you will see later in this chapter, clouds are good indicators also of what the weather holds. There are many different types of clouds, although just three types are enough to provide visible evidence of what is taking place, and what is to take place shortly. Cloud changes, in particular, are useful for signaling weather changes while you are out on the water. In fact, if you have been out sailing for many hours, and you do not have a radio on board, the clouds are probably the only indication you have of an impending weather change. We will see just how shortly.

WEATHER PATTERNS

Weather systems in the United States move from west to east. This general movement is caused by the westerlies—prevailing winds that result from the earth's rotation. In addition, the heating effect of the sun and the interaction of high- and low-pressure areas produce weather changes.

As you may know, the weather we experience is the result of alternating high- and low-pressure areas passing overhead. That is, "lows" are usually followed by "highs." When the pressure is high, the weather is generally good. On the other hand, the weather is usually poor when a low is centered overhead.

Highs and lows are characterized by a particular type of air movement. As the figure on page 72 shows, the wind blows in a clockwise direction around a high, but also toward the outside. This is called *anticyclonic rotation*. The wind around a low, on the other hand, blows in a counter-clockwise direction toward the low-pressure center. This movement is called *cyclonic rotation*. A hurricane is simply a cyclonic storm of great intensity. As the warm, moist air rotates toward the center of any low system, the

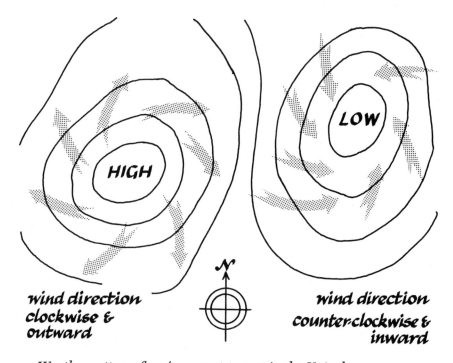

wind direction clockwise & outward

wind direction counter-clockwise & inward

Weather patterns flow from west to east in the United States, with high-pressure areas alternating with low-pressure areas. This diagram shows how the winds blow around lows and highs.

air begins to rise. But in rising it is cooled. Then, when sufficient cooling has occurred, moisture condenses and clouds and rain result.

A closer look at the figure will suggest one or two additional clues to the weather. For example, along the East Coast strong northeast winds usually mean increasing cloudiness and rain. In New England such storm systems are referred to as "nor'easters." When the wind then shifts to the northwest, it usually means the passage of a low and the approach of a high. Clearing generally follows, and fair weather can be expected until the next low arrives.

So far we have described the air mass movements that produce weather changes over very wide areas. The wind of a nor'easter and the brisk northwest breeze that follows passage of a cold front are results of these major air movements. On a smaller scale, the sailor can also look for two types of local breezes, both of which can affect his sailing pleasure. These two breezes are called the *land breeze* and the *sea breeze*.

Land and sea breezes occur near the coastline. Indeed, the story is that fore-and-aft rigs were originally developed in this country to take advantage of the land and sea breezes along our seacoasts and on the Great Lakes. These breezes develop because water and land differ in their capacity to absorb and hold heat. Water absorbs heat from the sun much more slowly than land, but it also holds the heat much longer. Let's see how this effect causes land and sea breezes. We'll start our description at a point in time when the water and land temperatures are about the same—an hour or so before midnight.

As the night hours pass, the land continues to cool. The water just offshore, however, does not lose heat as fast. The result is that around midnight the air above the water is warmer than the air above the adjacent land area. But warm air rises. Thus the air above the water rises, and the cooler air over the land area moves in be-

How a land breeze is generated. The warmer air above
the water rises, and the cooler air over the land moves
under it.

neath it. This cool air in motion off the land is the land
breeze. Of course, as the cool air comes in contact with
the warmer water, it is also warmed. It then rises, and
the cycle continues.

After sunrise, the land warms up rapidly. On a bright,
sunny day it is usually warmer than the adjacent water
sometime around noon. At this point a sea breeze begins.
The warm air over the land rises, and cooler air moves
off the water to take its place. Anyone who has been to
the beach on a bright, warm day is familiar with sea
breezes. They usually blow briskly through the afternoon, and then die down around sundown. The greater
the temperature difference between land and water, the
stronger the breeze.

Many sailors have learned to depend upon afternoon
sea breezes to get them home. On Long Island Sound, for

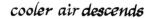

cooler air descends   warmed air rises

SEA BREEZE
begins at noon
cooler air   **ends at sundown**
above water   **strongest in late afternoon**

STEADY BREEZE   land is warmer
than water

*How a sea breeze is generated. The warmer air over the
land rises, then the air cooled above the water moves in
under it. Late-afternoon sea breezes are often a great
help in getting back to home port.*

example, the afternoon sea breeze from the south is prac-
tically a tradition. Local sailors call it the "homing"
breeze; they are greatly disappointed if it does not appear "on time" to get them into port before dusk. Sailboarders, however, should be cautious about counting on
the homing breeze. It is risky to take a craft as vulnerable
as a sailboard far off shore in the expectation that a late-
afternoon breeze will come up and bring the boat home.

FRONTS, CLOUDS, AND STORMS

With major air masses rotating around highs and lows,
contact between two masses of air with differing temperatures is inevitable. Such a collision is called a *front*.

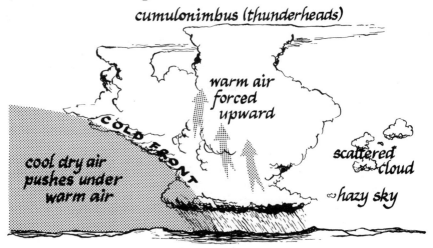

*A cold front exists when a mass of cold air pushes under
a mass of warmer air. As the warmer air then rises,
violent thunderstorms often develop.*

There are four types of front: *cold, warm, occluded,* and
stationary.

As far as the sailor is concerned, the cold front is the
most important, for it is usually accompanied by violent
thunderstorms. A cold front is produced when a cold air
mass meets and thrusts under a warm air mass. Because
the colder air is heavier, it stays close to the ground, but
forces the warm, moist air rapidly to high altitudes. As
the warm air rises and cools, its moisture condenses,
forming thunderhead clouds. Severe thunderstorms often
result.

A warm front results when warm air rides up and over
a mass of cold air. The warm air, usually laden with
moisture, then cools, and the moisture condenses. Cloudiness and rain are the result. Sometimes a fast-moving
cold front will overtake a warm front moving in the same

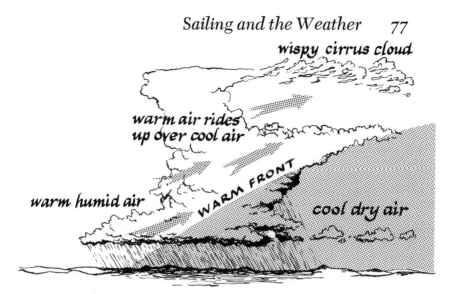

A warm front develops when a mass of warm air rides up and over a mass of cold air. As the warm air, usually laden with moisture, rises, it is cooled. The moisture then condenses, and widespread cloudiness and rain result.

direction. When this happens, the cold air in front of and behind the warm air forces the warm air upward. This is called an occluded front. Such fronts may behave as cold fronts, or warm fronts, or both. Finally, when a cold front and a warm front meet head on and interlock, the result is a stationary front. It helps to know the type of weather frontal conditions will bring. In particular, you should be wary of any approaching cold front, for the thunderstorms it usually brings are often very severe and dangerous.

Of the many different cloud types, three are of particular importance to the sailor. These are the *cumulonimbus,* or thunderhead; the *cumulus;* and the *cirrus* clouds. Cumulonimbus clouds are the massive vertical thunderhead clouds associated with the violent thunderstorms mentioned earlier. All sailors must learn to recognize

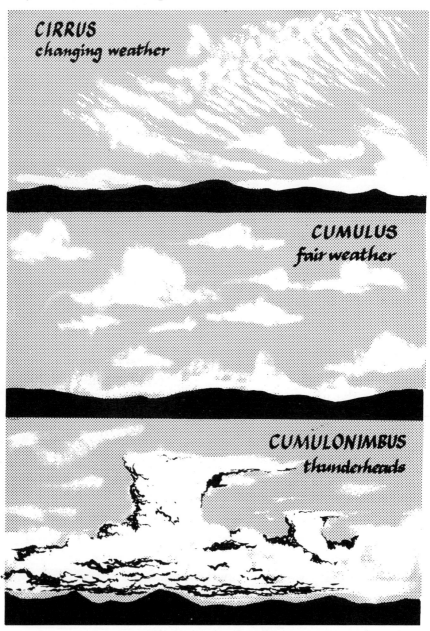

The cloud shapes and patterns you should learn to recognize. It is especially important that you learn to spot thunderheads before the thunderstorm arrives.

these clouds, for the storms they bring can be very dangerous to a boat under sail.

The typical thunderstorm occurs during the summer months, usually late in the day. These storms make their first appearance as a darkening sky, usually in the northwest. Often, however, the first warning of an approaching thunderstorm may be AM radio static. Static may develop up to ten hours prior to the storm itself. A sailboard is not the best place for a radio, but someone on the beach or dock should keep one available. Following the darkening sky, the typical anvil-shaped and towering thunderhead appears. The cloud is dark and "dirty" along its bottom, with violent wind gusts, heavy rain, and whitecaps underneath. The top is anvil-shaped, but sometimes the cloud is so tall this formation isn't visible. Very often these storms advance in a sharply defined front—an awesome sight to anyone who has witnessed it at sea.

When the storm hits, usually no more than a half hour after one sights the thunderhead, there will be violent winds from several different directions and usually drenching rain. In one thunderstorm we rode out at anchor, the rain was so heavy it was impossible to see the stern of the boat from the cabin—a distance of some seven feet! Waves are generally not a problem, for these storms come up too quickly to generate much wave action.

The winds in thunderstorms are so violent and erratic it is very important to prepare properly for the arrival of the storm. *Under no circumstances should you attempt to sail through a thunderstorm.* If you are close enough to shore—be it a sandy beach, a sheltered cove, or home port—get in as quickly as possible, and get the sails down. You should never be so careless that you are caught in a thunderstorm while out on a sailboard. If it

*There is no doubt about what this late-afternoon dark sky
means. A thunderstorm is on its way, and small-boat
sailors are getting back into home port as quickly as they
can. (Photo by Dorothy I. Crossley)*

should happen, however, there are a few things you can
and should do to protect yourself and your passengers.
First, make sure everyone on board is wearing a life
jacket. Second, drop the sails and lash them down se-
curely. Lash down the rudder and daggerboard also if
they are not locked in place. Third, hang on tight and
ride out the storm. If the boat is overturned, stay with
it. Remember, virtually all sailboards are unsinkable. It is
much safer to hang onto an overturned boat than to swim
for shore in a thunderstorm.

If the thunderstorms you are caught in are the result
of isolated masses of hot air rising into colder air, you can
expect them to pass over quickly. These are the typical
late-afternoon storms of a hot summer day. Storms associated with a cold front, however, may take longer to

clear out. As you may know, these storms spread out along the entire cold front. They are more violent than the local thunderstorm, but they can be avoided, for an approaching cold front is usually forecast well in advance.

Cumulus clouds are fair-weather clouds. These are the bright "cottony" clouds seen on fair, sunny days. They have softly rounded edges, but near the horizon they are flat along the bottom. As long as cumulus clouds are in the sky, there is little chance of any change in the weather. It pays to keep an eye on cumulus clouds, however. Sometimes one can grow tall enough to reach ele-

The brisk winds that follow the passage of a cold front are often ideal for getting a sailboard up on a plane. Note the fair-weather cumulus clouds. Such clouds often appear after a cold front has passed. (Photo by Dorothy I. Crossley)

vations where the temperature is below freezing. When this happens, the innocent fair-weather cumulus cloud can develop into the dangerous cumulonimbus thunderhead cloud.

Cirrus clouds generally indicate a change in weather, usually for the worse. These clouds are thin and wispy. A sky with cirrus clouds is often called a "mare's tail" sky, because of its similarity to the feathery wisps of a streaming horse's tail. Cirrus clouds occur at altitudes of twenty to twenty-five thousand feet. They often indicate cloudy, rainy weather within a day or so.

STORM WARNINGS

Always check the weather report before going out sailing. In addition, check for storm warnings at a nearby yacht club or marina. Administered by the U. S. Weather Bureau, storm warning stations are located along the East and West Coasts, on the Great Lakes, and in Hawaii and Puerto Rico. The warnings consist of flags or pennants for the daytime and lights for nighttime. There are four warnings: *small-craft, gale, storm,* and *hurricane.* You should commit these signals to memory, and never forget to check before going out sailing.

The most important warning for the sailboarder is the small-craft advisory. This signal, when posted, covers a wide range of wind and/or sea conditions. In addition, the term "small craft" includes boats of many different sizes and types. To be on the safe side, always get a detailed weather forecast before going out when the small-craft advisory pennant is flying. Wind and sea conditions may or may not be too severe for your boat—you won't be able to tell from the signal alone. It will be necessary to

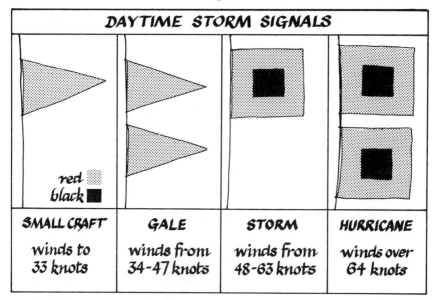

DAYTIME STORM SIGNALS			
red ▦ black ■			
SMALL CRAFT	GALE	STORM	HURRICANE
winds to 33 knots	winds from 34-47 knots	winds from 48-63 knots	winds over 64 knots

The daytime storm signals of the Weather Bureau Coastal Warning Display System. Be sure to get a complete weather forecast whenever small-craft advisories are displayed. It may be too rough for your boat.

match experience with a detailed weather report to estimate the danger correctly. For example, on a given day wind and sea conditions might be very hazardous for a twenty-foot centerboard boat or any sailboard, but merely exciting and stimulating for a twenty-foot keel boat.

TIDE AND CURRENT

A brief word about the tides and the water movements they cause is in order at this point. Strictly speaking, *tide* is the vertical rise and fall of a body of water. Tide is caused by the gravitational pull of the moon, and to a lesser extent that of the sun, on a body of water. When the sun and the moon are in line with the earth, their combined pull is greater. Hence, the tidal range is greater. Such tides are called *spring tides.* On the other hand, when the sun, moon, and earth form a right angle in space—that is, when they are not in a line—the tidal range is smallest. These tides are called *neap tides.*

Current is the horizontal flow of water. When the tide changes at high tide, and the water begins to drop, it can only drop by flowing horizontally out of or away from the bay or inlet it had flooded. Current caused by tidal changes is called *tidal current.* Sailboarders should learn the characteristics of the tidal current, if there is one, wherever they sail. Many a sailboard and its discouraged crew have been carried far off shore by an ebbing tidal current under light wind conditions.

The current of a river or stream is not associated in any way with the tide; it is caused by the earth's gravitational attraction only. Of course, many rivers that empty into the ocean experience tides. On the Connecticut River, for example, the effect of the tide is quite noticeable as far north as Hartford, a distance of some forty miles from the mouth of the river.

6. Safe Sailing Is the Best Sailing

WHENEVER WE READ or hear of a tragic accident that has taken place on the water, there is a tendency to think that it can't happen to us. Nothing could be farther from the truth. Accidents show no preference, unless it is to the habitually careless sailor. The careful sailor, on the other hand, can look forward to happy and rewarding hours on the water because he has made it a habit to prevent potential accidents before they have a chance to occur. This is the crux of the matter. Sailing, like other active sports, is not completely free of danger. It is, however, a sport whose dangerous elements can be controlled. The secret is to anticipate what might happen and then take preventive steps. This doesn't mean that you should be overly cautious. It does mean, however, that you should understand the capabilities of your boat, the sea and weather conditions you can expect to face, and your own resources.

SAFETY EQUIPMENT

Throughout this book we have stressed safe sailing practices as essential to getting the most pleasure out of your sailboard. At this point we want to bring the question of safety to a focus and review the essential equipment for a sailboard. Keep in mind that the Coast Guard does not require all of the items we will list. Its requirements are the legal limits only. The prudent sailboarder will supplement the required equipment with enough additional equipment to handle whatever conditions the boat can expect to meet.

To begin with, the law now requires that there be at least one Coast Guard-approved personal flotation device (PFD)—a life preserver—for each person on board a sailboard. Moreover, all persons who might expect to be on board or use the sailboard should be instructed in the use of the life preservers provided. No doubt many sailboarders will scoff at this requirement, and either forget the life preservers or lash then tightly to the mast. Such sailors could end up sorry for their actions, for the Coast Guard has vowed to enforce this rule. In one case, for example, a sailboarder was arrested because the life preservers were *not available*—they were lashed to the mast (and would be difficult to remove if needed in a hurry). Despite the fact that this arresting officer may have been overzealous, this is an indication that the authorities intend strict enforcement of the life preserver rule.

Many sailboards have a small built-in storage locker, or *cuddy*, forward or aft of the cockpit. If your boat does not have such a compartment, there is very little you can do about additional safety equipment. Under these circumstances, you should stay close to shore or within hailing distance of help should you need it. If your boat does have a cuddy, however, a few additional items will come in handy. Toss in a sponge or absorbent rag for completely drying the cockpit. If one will fit, include a telescoping paddle for those times when the wind dies.

It's wise also to carry some tools and spare parts. A good knife, a pair of pliers, a screwdriver, and a flashlight may come in handy some day (or night). Take along extra shackles, blocks, screws, or whatever other fittings you could not get along without. Place any spare parts or tools that might rust or corrode in a watertight bag or container. Otherwise, they are certain to get wet if the boat is dumped. Would you be prepared if the sail were to tear? Probably not. Take along a small sewing kit, as well as some sail-repair tape, and you will not be stranded in some strange place away from home port.

DROWNPROOFING

The great majority of drownings associated with boating accidents need not occur. Too often sailors thrown into the water forget or refuse to stay with the boat. In addition, many have never attempted to learn how to stay afloat fully clothed, or even how to disrobe in the

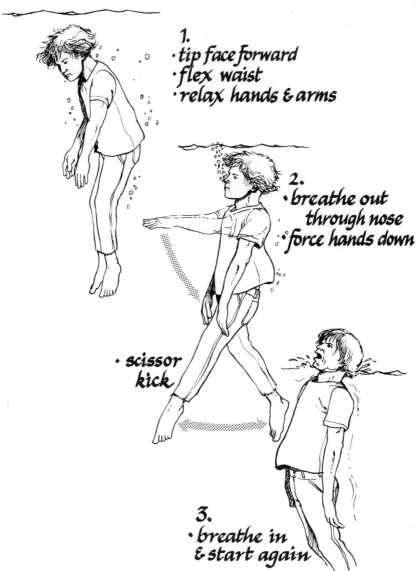

1.
- tip face forward
- flex waist
- relax hands & arms

2.
- breathe out through nose
- force hands down

- scissor kick

3.
- breathe in & start again

How the technique of "drownproofing" works. This procedure for staying afloat for very long time periods is based on the fact that with very few exceptions the body will float vertically when the lungs are fully inflated. See the text for details.

water. These are important, of course, because sailors often wear bulky clothes to guard against the elements.

Drownproofing is a technique of floating that all sailboarders should know. It is particularly valuable, for it allows the person in the water to remain afloat for long periods of time with little or no energy expended. Moreover, it is a technique that can be quite successfully carried out even when fully clothed. If you are not a reasonably good swimmer, you should never sail without wearing a life jacket. In addition, you should not attempt to learn the drownproofing technique unless you are a good swimmer, and under no circumstances should you attempt to learn it alone. Work with another competent swimmer, and practice by the side of a pool or close to the edge of a dock. Wear just a bathing suit at first. If you have any doubt about your swimming ability, seek professional help from a qualified water safety instructor.

The floating or resting position, also called the front survival position, consists of the body being erect in the water, with the waist slightly flexed and the face tipped forward; the hands and arms dangle in a relaxed fashion. The breath is held in this position for four or five seconds. At this point, in order to raise the head above water for a breath of air, the arms and legs are used to propel the body upward. The hands are forced downward accompanied by a scissor kick. This lifts the body sufficiently for an inhalation. During the motion upward, while the face is still submerged, a full exhalation takes place through the nose. If this is done correctly, the head needs to be out of the water only long enough for an inhalation. After taking the fresh breath of air, the head is tipped forward again, and the body is allowed to return to the original floating position. Rhythm is very important. Once an easy, smooth cycle has been mastered, the swimmer can float this way for very long periods of time indeed.

Mastering this skill will teach you a great deal about what type of clothing to wear while sailing. As you practice with clothing on, you will discover that lightweight clothing that allows maximum movement is the best. We hope that you will never have to use this technique in seriousness, for in the event of a capsize a life preserver should be right at hand. We hope also that should you find yourself in the water with a capsized boat, you will be able to stay with it and wait for help. On the other hand, the day may come when you are in the water separated from your boat. Your chances for survival will be much greater if you have made yourself "drownproof."

RULES OF THE ROAD

One of the first things you will notice when you begin sailing is the traffic. America's recreational waterways are becoming more and more crowded every year. Unfortunately, along with the crowding there has been a noticeable increase in the number of accidents. Thus, to enjoy sailing and to avoid accidents it becomes necessary to thoroughly master the traffic rules that govern the movements of boats. These rules are called the *rules of the road;* their fundamental purpose is to avoid collisions. The rules apply to all types of boats, and cover all of the possible types of meetings that can take place between two boats. In all of these instances the rules determine the boat that is *privileged* and the boat that is *burdened*. A privileged boat has the *right of way*, and is entitled to, and to a large extent is obligated to maintain course and

*Which boat has the right of way? Even more important,
do both skippers* know *who has the right of way, and is
the appropriate action being taken? If you don't know the
rules of the road, situations such as this one can lead to
nasty accidents. (Photo by Dorothy I. Crossley)*

speed. The burdened boat must look out for the privileged boat; it must alter course and/or speed so that it
does not interfere with the privileged boat.

In almost all instances, a sailboat under sail alone has
the right of way over a powerboat. This means that powerboats should stay clear of sailboats at all times. The important exceptions to this rule are as follows. A sailboat
overtaking and passing a powerboat (or any boat, for
that matter) is burdened; it must stay clear. Another exception refers to meetings between sailboats and very

large powered vessels in restricted channels. Neither sail-boats nor powerboats under sixty-five feet in length can claim the right of way over large, powered vessels that can navigate only inside a restricted channel. The safest application of this rule is to attempt to stay clear of all other vessels when sailing in a narrow channel. As we mentioned earlier, this situation will probably only occur if you attempt to tack upwind in a narrow channel. Finally, remember that all other vessels, including sailboats under sail alone, must stay clear of fishing vessels using nets or lines or trawls.

An informal rule that you should take to heart and employ whenever you are in doubt is as follows: *Don't press your advantage!* With the very large number of in-experienced boatmen now crowding the waterways, you cannot count on the other man knowing the rules or correctly anticipating your intentions. We repeat: If you are in doubt about the situation, make every attempt to stay clear. Such common sense and courtesy will go a long way toward making your hours on the water both happy and safe.

RULES FOR BOATS UNDER SAIL ALONE

As you become familiar with the following rules, you will note that they favor the boat that is sailing close-hauled—that is, the privileged boat is the one that is closehauled. This ruling dates back to the days of the square-riggers, vessels that sailed poorly to windward. Sailing closehauled was thus favored by the seafaring men who originally established the rules of the road.

The rules are as follows. Whenever two sailing vessels are approaching each other in such a way that there is

A vessel that is running free shall keep out of the way of a vessel that is closehauled.

wind aft
KEEP CLEAR

closehauled
PRIVILEGED

A vessel closehauled on the port tack shall keep out of the way of a vessel that is closehauled on the starboard tack.

both closehauled

port tack

starboard tack

KEEP CLEAR   PRIVILEGED

When both are running free with the wind on different sides, the vessel with the wind on the port side shall keep out of the way of the other.

running free

wind to port   wind to starboard
KEEP CLEAR   PRIVILEGED

When both are running free with the wind on the same side, the vessel that is to the windward shall keep out of the way of the vessel that is to the leeward.

running free ~   wind on same side

to windward
KEEP CLEAR

to leeward
PRIVILEGED

A vessel that has the wind aft shall keep out of the way of the other vessel.

running free
KEEP CLEAR

PRIVILEGED

You will most certainly encounter other sailboats when out sailboarding, so learn the rules of the road for when both vessels are under sail alone. Note that these rules favor the boat that is sailing closehauled.

a risk of collision, one of the vessels must stay clear. The possible situations and the rules are:

1. *A boat that is running free will stay clear of a boat that is closehauled.* The boat running free is burdened.

2. *A boat closehauled on the port tack will stay clear of a boat closehauled on the starboard tack.* The boat on the port tack is burdened.

3. *When both boats are running free, but with the wind on different sides, the boat that has the wind on its port side will stay clear of the other.* Again, the boat on the port tack is burdened. Remember it this way: port, red, danger, burdened.

4. *When boats are running free, with the wind on the same side, the boat that is to windward still stay clear of the boat that is to leeward.* In this case, the boat that is upwind is burdened.

5. *A boat that has the wind aft will stay clear of the other vessel.*

It is very important that you learn these rules well and that you apply them. At the same time keep in mind that many boatmen will not know the rules and that you will be forced to assume the responsibility for preventing accidents. By all means be upset when you observe failure to abide by the rules of the road. And you will observe such failure. We can only say that education is the answer to this type of problem. You may find yourself in a position someday to help by participating in either U. S. Power Squadron or Coast Guard Auxiliary safe-boating programs. We hope that you will respond when the opportunity presents itself. Also keep in mind that the rules given above *do not apply* to sailboats in a race. The racing rules differ somewhat from the rules above, and apply only to the boats in the race; they do not apply to boats that happen onto a racing course.

RULES FOR BOATS UNDER POWER

Many small sailboats use outboard engines as auxiliary power. Whenever a sailboat is being powered by an engine—even if the sails are up—the boat is a motorboat according to the law. Boats powered in this manner—and, of course, all other craft powered by some type of machinery—are motorboats and must follow the motorboat rules of the road. You should know these rules, which differ from the sailing rules. They are as follows:

1. *Two motorboats approaching each other head on should pass port side to port side.* When the skipper of one of the boats alters course to starboard to honor this

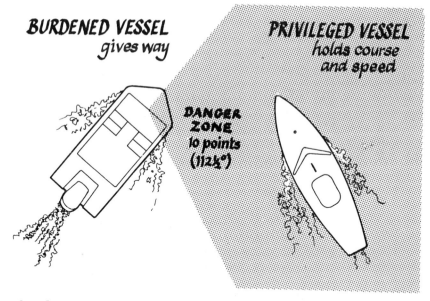

The "danger zone" rule for motorboats. Any power boat that has another boat in its danger zone must give way. This could mean altering course, stopping, or even reversing if necessary.

rule, he should give one short blast on his horn. The other skipper should then acknowledge by returning the single short blast. In the event two boats are approaching each other and will pass starboard to starboard, two short blasts on the horn should be given to indicate that course is being altered to port. Wherever possible, the boats should pass port side to port side, although instances do occur when it is more practical to pass starboard side to starboard side.

2. *A motorboat having another in its danger zone (from dead ahead to two points abaft the starboard beam) must stay clear.* The figure on page 95 shows how the "danger zone" rule applies. It may even be necessary to stop or reverse direction to stay clear.

3. *Any boat leaving a slip, or a berth at a dock, has no rights until it is entirely clear.* This means that the boat leaving the slip or dock must consider itself burdened until it is completely clear of the dock and in open water.

Additional horn signals you should learn to recognize are (a) three short blasts—my boat is proceeding astern, and (b) four or more blasts—danger! (either an emergency or failure to understand another vessel's signals).

WHAT BUOYS DO FOR THE SAILOR

In general, two types of buoys are in use on U.S. waters: unlighted buoys without sounds, and buoys that have sound and/or light. Buoys mark the presence of a channel in a systematic way that makes it very clear to a sailor where he should steer his boat. This system is based on color, buoy shape, and numbering.

Imagine you are entering a channel or harbor from

seaward. As you proceed up the channel, you will note that the buoys on the right-hand side are red; they are also marked with even numbers. The use of *red* for buoys on the *right* of a channel has given rise to a simple memory device: think *red, right, returning,* and you will always remember to leave the red buoys to starboard as you enter a channel, harbor, or river from seaward. Of course, when you are going toward the sea you would leave the red buoys to port.

The left-hand side of a channel is marked by black buoys with odd numbers. Buoy shape also distinguishes the right from the left side of a channel. The red buoys on the right are conical in shape; they are called *nun* buoys. The black buoys on the left are cylindrical; they are called *can* buoys. Two other color schemes are in use. In one, black-and-white vertical stripes on an un-numbered buoy mark the middle of a channel. Small boats may pass close by, and on either side of this type of buoy. In the other color scheme, black-and-red horizontal bands on a buoy indicate a channel junction or some type of underwater obstruction inside the channel itself. These buoys should be given a wide berth. They may be passed on either side, but the color of the top band indicates the preferred channel. In the figure on page 98, for example, the red-and-black junction buoy's top band is red. Thus, the preferred channel is to the left of the buoy; the boat leaves the buoy's red top to starboard.

Buoys that have special importance to the navigator are lighted, equipped with sound, or both. Such buoys mark the entrance to a harbor; they are used also to mark a bend in a channel. To get some idea of the importance of light and sound in buoys, just consider the following situations. You are sailing on open water at night, and

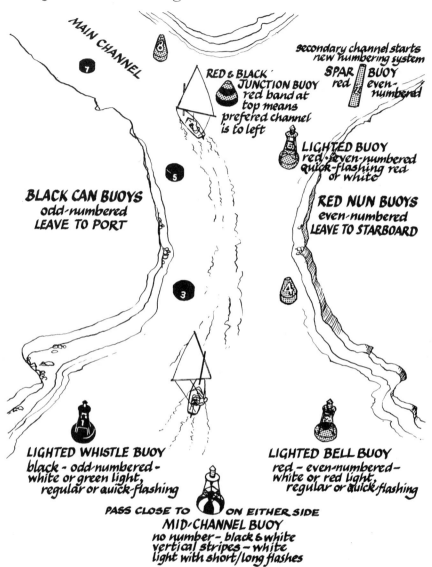

MAIN CHANNEL

secondary channel starts
new numbering system

SPAR BUOY
red even-
numbered

RED & BLACK
JUNCTION BUOY
red band at
top means
prefered channel
is to left

LIGHTED BUOY
red - even-numbered
quick-flashing red
or white

BLACK CAN BUOYS
odd-numbered
LEAVE TO PORT

RED NUN BUOYS
even-numbered
LEAVE TO STARBOARD

LIGHTED WHISTLE BUOY
black - odd-numbered -
white or green light,
regular or quick-flashing

LIGHTED BELL BUOY
red - even-numbered -
white or red light,
regular or quick-flashing

PASS CLOSE TO ON EITHER SIDE
MID-CHANNEL BUOY
no number - black & white
vertical stripes - white
light with short/long flashes

BUOY NUMBERS INCREASE TOWARD HEAD OF NAVIGATION

*How buoys are used on U.S. waters. Learn the
significance of the color, the shape, and the numbers used
on buoys, and finding your way will be a relatively
simple task.*

want to enter a sheltered harbor. As you approach land its mass is solid black to the eye. No landmarks are discernible. The entrance to the harbor, however, is marked by two lighted buoys. The one on the right will have either a red or a white light, with regular or quick flashing. The buoy on the left will have either a green or a white light, again with regular or quick flashing. A chart will tell you the color of the lights and also the nature of the flashing. Your job is to spot the buoys, and then sail cautiously between them to enter the harbor.

In the second situation, suppose you are caught in fog, but know the general direction toward a sheltered harbor you wish to enter. Reference to a chart will tell you immediately if the harbor entrance is marked by bell or whistle buoys. With this information, you should proceed very cautiously toward the harbor entrance, following the sound of the buoys. Go very slowly and with great care in fog. You must be alert constantly to the possibility of collision. In addition, because sound behaves very strangely in fog, you must be alert to the possibility of straying away from the center of the harbor entrance.

One final comment about buoys is necessary. Every effort is made to maintain buoys in good condition and in their proper positions. This does not mean, however, that they will always be correctly placed. They may be adrift, off their charted positions due to heavy storms, unusual tides, and collisions, or even missing entirely. Because of these possibilities, a reasonable distance should always be allowed between the boat and a buoy when the buoy is passed.

COURTESY AFLOAT

All sailors have equal rights and privileges when on the water. By the same token, however, all sailors carry the responsibility to respect the rights of their fellow boatmen. This means much more than obeying the rules of the road to the letter. It involves anticipating the desires and movements of the other skipper's boat and then taking action to respect his rights.

In order to cover as many courtesy situations as possible, we will list them as a series of do's and don'ts. This will give you a quick reference for courtesy problems, and permit us to make the best use of available space.

DO stay clear of boats that are racing. If you must sail through a racing fleet, DO pass astern of all boats racing closehauled, and DO keep to leeward of all boats running free.

DO go to the help of fellow boatmen in distress. This is a universal obligation. Always remember that tomorrow you may need help.

DON'T go aboard another boat or borrow a sailboard until you have checked with the owner.

DO be courteous and friendly to boating people. You will find that an outgoing, friendly manner will be received cordially by most boating folk.

DO stay clear of channels and traffic lanes in strange anchorages.

DON'T be a litterbug. DO save your garbage and trash in suitable containers until you can dispose of it ashore.

DON'T butt in with unasked-for advice while aboard someone else's boat. Follow the wishes of the skipper while you are his guest. He expects to behave the same way aboard your boat.

DON'T abuse your right-of-way privilege over powerboats. As pointed out earlier, it is the better part of valor to give way in any situation that might endanger or otherwise inconvenience the powerboat skipper.

DO learn to recognize the skindiver's flag and stay clear of skindiving activities. The flag is bright orange-red with a diagonal white stripe.

DON'T tie up to government navigation buoys, or land at a private dock or float except in an emergency. The law forbids anyone to tie up at a navigation aid maintained by the Coast Guard, so think twice before tying up at a buoy, even in an emergency.

Scamper, the sailboard whose construction from a kit is described in this chapter.

7. Build Your Own Sailboard

MANY WOULD-BE sailboarders find that they cannot afford to buy a new or used sailboard. This is unfortunate, but there are other options. One is to seek out boat rental establishments that handle sailboards. Such firms are becoming more numerous each year. Look in areas served by sandy beaches open to the public and having little or no surf. Often it is possible to get sailing lessons along with the sailboard.

Another option, one that involves reasonable cost and the opportunity to use basic handyman skills, is to build your own sailboard. This is a fine task for the winter season, for example, for a father-and-son team, or perhaps for a couple of brothers or friends determined to get out on the water. There are just two ways to build your own sailboard, unless you include designing the boat yourself. These are (1) assembling preformed parts supplied in a kit, and (2) working from a set of plans. In this chapter we will briefly describe each of these methods. You won't be able to build a boat from what you find here, but you will get a good idea of what each method involves.

FROM A KIT

The Fiberglas Scamper, supplied by Luger Industries, Inc., Burnsville, Minnesota, is a typical kit boat. Assembly of the Scamper requires no more than a week of evenings, at the most. When the kit package arrives, it will contain all of the needed hardware and fittings, spars, sail, and lines, the parts needed to build the daggerboard and rudder and tiller assembly, and most important, the molded Fiberglas hull, deck, cockpit, and support assembly for the daggerboard and mast. This part stabilizes the hull and deck as well. Refer to the figure on the next page, which shows the major parts, as construction of the hull is described.

To assemble the boat, just a few simple skills are required. The surfaces of all parts to be joined must be sanded clean and smooth. Two or three openings must be cut in the Fiberglas using a drill and keyhole saw. Holes for screws must be drilled and occasionally countersunk prior to setting the screws. A few wood parts must be cut to size. Many joints and seams must be Fiberglas-bonded using glass matte and a liquid mixture of resin and hardener. Silicone sealant must be applied at certain points to prevent water from entering the hull. And finally, the mahogany daggerboard, rudder, and tiller must be sanded, stained, and varnished before final assembly. With the complete instructions provided, assembly of Scamper or a similar boat is well within the capabilities of the average handyman or youngster who has had some experience using hand tools.

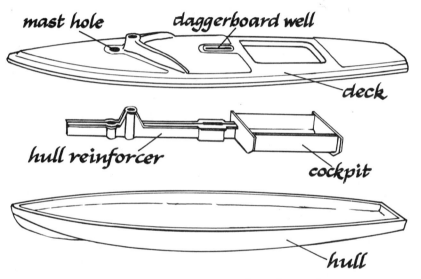

The major parts supplied in the Scamper kit. The cockpit must be assembled, and the hull reinforcer comes as matched facing parts that must be joined together.

The first task in the assembly of the hull is sandpapering the edges of all Fiberglas parts to a smooth surface. This is done to remove irregularities and protrusions. As you may know, the rough edges of molded Fiberglas parts are capable of producing nasty cuts and lacerations. Next, it is necessary to cut openings in the deck and hull bottom for the daggerboard. The hole for the mast in the deck then follows. The shapes of these openings may be premarked in the Fiberglas. If not, they must be transferred to the Fiberglas surface by means of templates provided with the instructions.

Assembly of the cockpit is next. First, the ends are cut out. They are then fastened to the central piece of the cockpit using stainless steel sheet metal screws and silicone sealant. The hull reinforcer follows. This part is supplied in two halves. Matching surfaces on the two halves are sanded smooth and clean, and the parts are then fitted together and fastened using bolts and silicone sealant.

At this point the hull bottom, cockpit, hull reinforcer, and deck must be fitted to each other. Some sanding may be needed to produce a perfect fit among the parts. Patience, careful measurement, and precise trimming are the watchwords here. If a good fit between the parts is not obtained at this stage of assembly, the hull may not stand up to the stresses and strains it will be subjected to when in use. Keep in mind that sailboard hulls tend to be banged about quite a bit, and that the better the fit between the hull parts the stronger the hull will be.

The next step is to fasten the hull reinforcer to the bottom of the hull and the cockpit to the underside of the deck. In the top figure on page 107, the centerline string is used to correctly align the top of the hull reinforcer. The part is taped in place with the daggerboard opening properly lined up under the string, and then bonded to the bottom of the hull with resin-saturated Fiberglas matte. A similar procedure is followed to bond the cockpit to the underside of the deck. A wood cockpit support and four wood cushion blocks are then bonded in place on the bottom of the cockpit. It will take four or five hours or more for the resin to cure, depending on temperature and humidity. Nothing should be moved until the resin has cured completely.

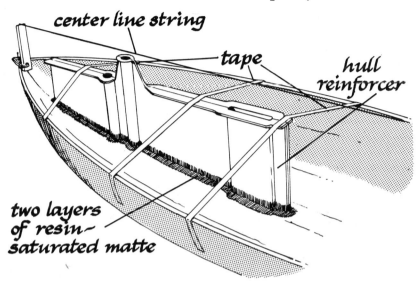

After the two halves of the hull reinforcer have been joined, the part is mounted in the bottom of the hull by means of resin-saturated Fiberglas matte.

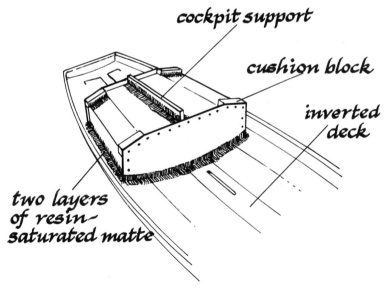

The assembled cockpit is bonded to the underside of the deck with Fiberglas matte.

After the Fiberglas bonds have thoroughly cured, the deck and hull hardware is fastened in place. Many of these parts are fastened down with machine screws, but some are bolted in place. Wherever bolts are used, the holes must be sealed with silicone compound to prevent leakage. If your kit included flotation foam, this is the time to install it. The foam pieces are cut to size and installed in the open areas of the hull bottom.

The final step in assembly of the hull is joining the deck to the hull bottom. The deck is dropped in place on top of the hull bottom, fitted correctly, and then fastened using machine screws after sealant has been placed

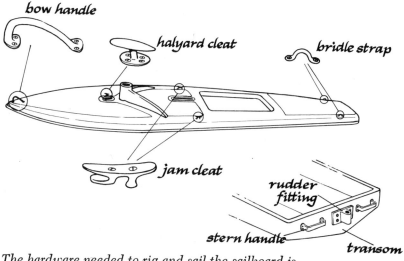

The hardware needed to rig and sail the sailboard is added before the deck and hull are joined together.

around the daggerboard and mast openings. Screws are spaced around the daggerboard and mast holes and completely around the lip of the deck where it overlaps the top of the hull bottom. At this point the hull is turned over and sealant is installed completely around the hull in the space between the lip of the deck and the top rim of the hull bottom.

After the deck and hull have been fastened together, silicone sealant is used to make the seam watertight. Cross-sectional detail is shown in (b). It is necessary also to seal the gaps around the daggerboard opening.

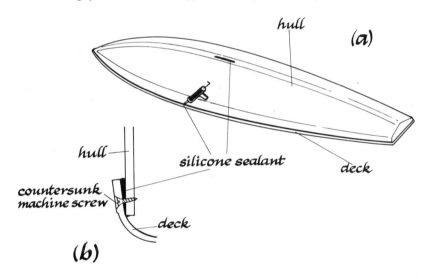

It is necessary also to seal any gaps where the bottom of the daggerboard well in the hull reinforcer lines up with the hole in the bottom of the hull.

To complete the boat, the rudder, tiller, and daggerboard must be finished and assembled. This involves some sandpapering, the application of stain and varnish, and final assembly of the parts. The daggerboard, of course, is simply dropped into the daggerboard well when you are sailing. The rudder and tiller assembly, however, must be mounted on the transom of the boat.

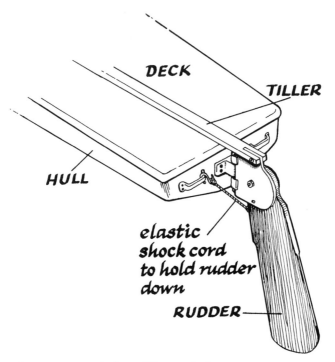

Close-up view of the rudder and tiller assembly mounted on the transom.

All that now remains is to assemble the spars (the boom and gaff) and mast, fasten the sail to the two spars, attach the bridle to the hull and rig the sheet line, and then mount the mast. The figure opposite shows the spars, mast, and sail in relation to each other. For a diagram of a complete lateen-rigged sailboard such as Scamper, refer back to page 102.

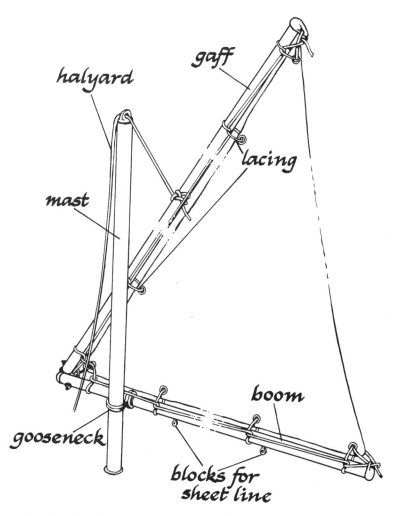

How the sail is laced to the boom and gaff on Scamper, and the correct position of the halyard on the boom for raising the sail.

FROM PLANS

Building a boat from plans is a bit more time-consuming and difficult than assembling a kit boat, largely because more detailed work and finer skills are called for.

GLEN L 10

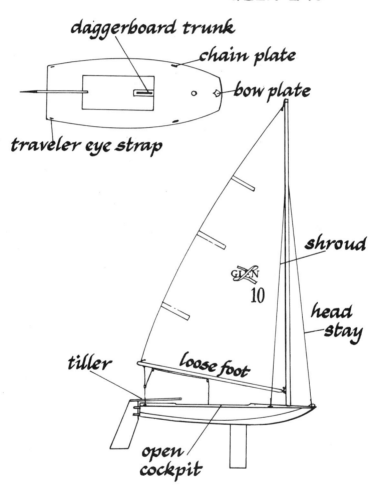

Features of the Glen L 10, a Marconi cat-rigged scow-type sailboard that is built from full-sized plans.

Nevertheless, many prospective boat builders prefer to work from plans, feeling that they are more deeply involved in bringing the craft into existence, and therefore can take greater pride in their handiwork. Thus the plans approach may be for you! If you've never actually constructed a boat from plans, however, the description that follows should help you to decide.

The boat whose construction we will describe is the Glen L 10. Plans for this boat are provided by Glen L Marine Designs, Bellflower, California. Glen L provided the photographs in this section also. The Glen L 10 is a nine-foot, eleven-inch-long scow-type sailboard with a Marconi cat rig. The complete plan set includes full-size patterns for the frames, transom, stem, side planking, rudder, daggerboard trunk, and bow piece of the hull. A fully illustrated instruction booklet is provided also.

The instructions for constructing the hull of the Glen L 10 begin with general specifications for lumber type and grade, fastenings, and gluing requirements. Instructions are then given for transferring the full-size patterns to the lumber stock. The patterns are not cut out. Instead, they are transferred to the stock using carbon paper or by pin-pricking through the plan template and into the stock at close intervals. In either case, the shape of the part is outlined on the stock and then cut out.

Assembly begins after all of the parts have been cut out. A first step is assembly of the stem. This part is put together by situating the pieces in place over the full-size pattern. Aligning the parts on the pattern is required to fasten them in the correct position. Other parts that must be put together prior to assembly of the hull itself include the frames, the transom, the daggerboard trunk, and the side planking. After the dagger-

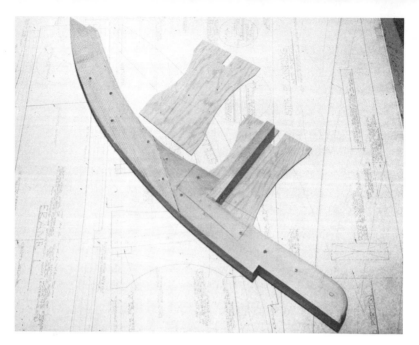

The stem is assembled by laying the parts out on the full-sized pattern.

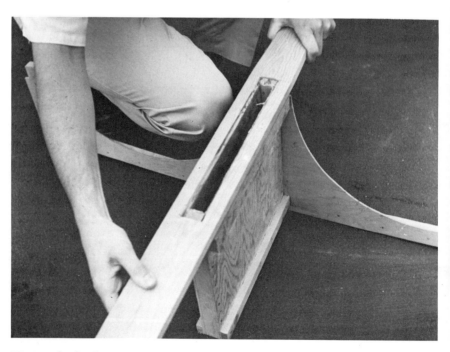

Fitting the keel opening over the bottom of the daggerboard trunk.

board trunk has been assembled, the opening in the keel through which the daggerboard will pass is cut out. The ends of the keel are left long so they can be fitted accurately to the stem and transom later.

Final assembly of the hull begins after all of the hull parts have been preassembled. These parts are shown laid out in the figure on this page. For the rest of the assembly procedure, follow the steps in the text beneath the photographs on the next four pages.

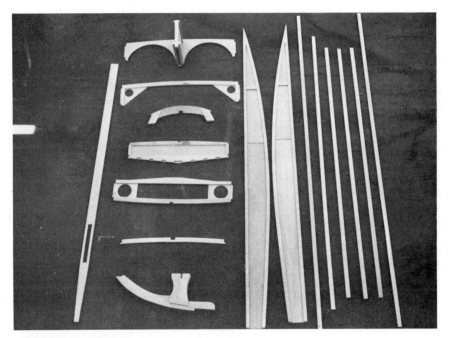

The preassembled hull parts prior to final assembly. From the left, the long members are the keel, the side planks, and the battens. From the top, the remaining parts are the daggerboard trunk, a frame, the bow piece, the transom, two frames, and the stem.

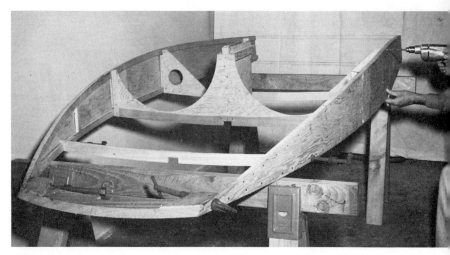

Assembly of the frames, side planks, bow piece, and transom is carried out on top of two saw horses, with the hull upside down. The side planks are fastened and clamped to the bow piece. They are then fitted to and sprung around each frame, working progressively toward the stern. Note the cord at the stern holding the planks in position.

The stem and keel assembly are now fitted into place. The keel must be cut to length to fit into the stem and transom properly. As shown, the keel is being fastened in place around the opening of the daggerboard trunk. All mated parts on this hull are joined using a hard-setting glue plus bronze or hot dipped galvanized iron fastenings.

The long strips shown being fastened in this photo are called battens. These strips lend longitudinal support to the hull bottom. They are notched into the transom, fastened down on the first frame forward of the transom, and then float free as they extend forward. When the bottom planking is added, fastening screws are driven through it and into the battens.

In laying down the bottom planking, the uncut plywood sheet is first clamped along the stem and keel. The shape of the hull is then marked and the excess cut away to give a perfect fit. The panel is then reapplied to the bottom of the boat and fastened progressively along the center line of the stem and keel.

When the bottom planking has been completed, the hull
is turned over and the interior treated with an antirot
chemical and/or marine paint. The longitudinal stringers
that provide support for the deck are then added. Note
the chain plates—the steel straps to which the shrouds
are fastened—on either side of the hull about 2.5 feet aft
of the bow.

After carefully measuring and cutting to size, the deck
planking is fastened down the same way the bottom
planking was secured. The deck pieces are carefully butt
joined prior to fastening to make sure they fit together
perfectly. Upon completion, the hull is trimmed and all
imperfections filled with a hard-setting putty. It can then
be either painted or Fiberglas applied.

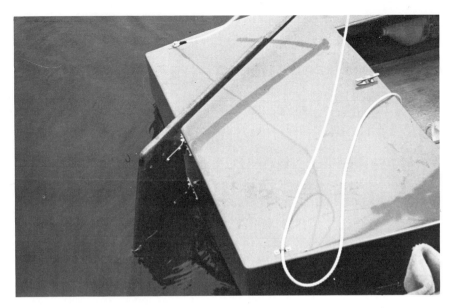

This close-up view of the stern area shows the rudder and tiller assembly, plus the manner in which the bridle for the main sheet is rigged. When the bridle has been adjusted to the desired length, the free end is fastened at the cleat mounted on the deck just aft of the cockpit. Note the tiller extension used when hiking out to windward.

The forward end of the cockpit, showing the mahogany trim, the floorboards on either side of the daggerboard trunk, and the cam cleat for the sheet line. Note the block just aft of the mast step and the cleat on the deck for the halyard. The pin on top of the daggerboard trunk passes through the bracket holding the cam cleat and into the daggerboard to hold it down in place.

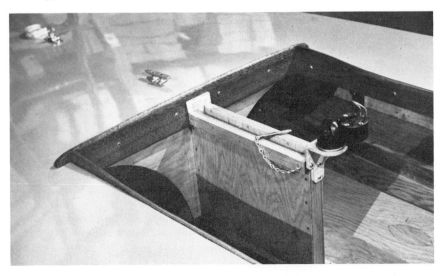

Following completion of the hull, the daggerboard and rudder and tiller assembly must be constructed, all hardware must be mounted on the boat, and the mast stepped and rigged. A completed boat is shown under sail in the photo here. As this photo clearly demonstrates, the Glen L 10 is a lively and fast boat. This craft, or something like it, may very well be just the boat for you.

8. Caring for Your Sailboard

ALTHOUGH THIS IS the last chapter of *Sailboarding*, it is by no means the least important. Just as the sheer fun of sailing is partially counterbalanced by the inevitable, if minor, element of danger, the enjoyment of well-maintained equipment is offset by the need for year-round maintenance. There is no escaping it. The elements and hard use combine to take a heavy toll on paint, varnish, gel coat, rigging, and sails unless continual efforts are made to keep a craft in top shape.

There are two aspects to caring for your sailboat. One has to do with where you will keep it. Many small-boat owners cartop or trailer their boats, while others use the facilities of a yacht club, marina, or boatyard. Many sailboards, however, are stored on the beach between outings all season long.

Despite the fact that some sailors may not be old enough to drive a car, we will discuss trailering in some detail. What we have to say will come in handy later, when today's young readers are driving.

The second aspect of caring for your boat has to do with maintenance. As you will discover, this is a year-round chore. There is no need, however, to look at maintenance with any sense of foreboding. When the necessary upkeep chores on a boat are performed in a routine manner the year round, these responsibilities

Because of their size and light weight, sailboards are easily cartopped.

become a natural but not burdensome part of boating. Of course, if your boat is an old "clunker," you may find maintenance occupying all of your time and effort, to the exclusion of any sailing fun.

As pointed out earlier, modern methods of construction using the most up-to-date materials have given us durable and relatively easy-to-maintain hulls, rigging, and sails. Hulls of Fiberglas, stainless steel rigging, aluminum spars, and sails of Dacron and nylon are relatively maintenance-free. Nylon and Dacron lines have replaced manila lines, also reducing the cost of operating a boat. Finally, modern antifouling paints keep a boat's bottom relatively clean compared with the situation just a few years ago. Bottom paint, however, is not needed if you store your sailboard out of the water between outings.

TRAILERING

One of the great advantages of owning a small sailboat, especially a sailboard, is that it need not be moored in a permanent anchorage or berthed in a slip. Instead, it can be stored anywhere you like on a trailer. Another advantage is that virtually all bodies of water that have launching ramps are available for sailing fun. Small boats kept in the water, on the other hand, are confined to the immediate area of home port.

Selecting a trailer for a boat requires careful thought. The trailer should provide support in the right places, so that the hull will not sag and lose its shape. With respect to the size of the trailer, follow this rule of thumb: Take the total weight of the boat fully equipped; if this figure is within one hundred pounds of the rated capacity of a trailer, choose the next larger trailer. A well-designed trailer will meet all local and state regulations and will provide good riding comfort with maximum safety in the towing car. Of great importance, dry launching with a minimum of physical effort should be possible. If you are in doubt, consult a dealer who is familiar with the different types of trailers and what they are designed to do. Buying a trailer is somewhat like buying tires; safety and reliability depend on quality.

Load distribution is an important factor in how well a boat on a trailer will ride. In general, the boat's center of gravity should be a bit forward of the trailer wheels. This will produce sufficient weight at the tongue of the trailer—something in excess of one hundred pounds. Take care to adjust this bumper-weight figure. If tongue weight is too great, the rear of the car will be forced down. If it is too little, the trailer will bob up and down at the rear bumper and produce a very uneven and unsafe ride.

A number of special precautionary measures when driving are necessary with a trailer following behind. First, check the trailer regulations to make sure your rig complies for all of the states within which you plan to travel. For example, you will probably need a rear light that includes a brake signal and directional signals. Launch only at approved hard-surfaced ramps to avoid getting your trailer and car stuck in sand or mud. When on the road, remember that you are carrying an extra-heavy load and that a greater stopping distance is required. Also remember to swing wide when passing and to allow extra room up ahead.

Most drivers experience their greatest difficulty when backing a trailer. Some practice is needed, of course, but if you remember to turn the steering wheel opposite to the direction in which you want the rear of the trailer to turn, you should minimize this difficulty. For example, to turn the rear of the trailer to the left, the steering wheel is turned to the right. Try it, but practice in a

Many sailboard owners trailer their boats, thus opening up any accessible body of water to sailing pleasure.

light-traffic area such as an empty parking lot before attempting to launch a boat.

There are certain steps to follow when launching a sailboard from a trailer. First, step the mast and then fasten the stays and shrouds, if your boat's rig includes them. Make sure that the mast is positioned properly. Next, attach the sails, but do not raise them until after the boat is in the water. To launch the boat, bring the trailer to the water at right angles to the shoreline, and be careful not to back down too far. There is nothing more embarrassing than a half-sunk stalled car and trailer.

Once the boat is in the water, getting away may still be a bit of a problem. It will be necessary to hoist the sails and get the boat into water deep enough for the daggerboard and rudder. The wind, of course, is a factor in getting away successfully. If the wind is onshore—that is, blowing in toward the shore—the problem is to get the boat into deep enough water to beat away from the shore.

One simple, although not very seamanlike technique, is simply to paddle the boat out into deep enough water before raising the sail, lowering the daggerboard, and attaching the rudder and tiller. If you elect to do this, be sure to point the bow into the wind before raising the sail.

SPRING CARE

Many sailors look forward in the spring to just dropping the boat in and taking off. This is a mistake. After the long winter storage period, either indoors or outside, a sailboard requires certain work before it can be put in the water. If you have performed all of the necessary fall lay-up chores conscientiously, getting your boat back on the water is an invigorating and satisfying activity. If you neglected those fall tasks, however, you will probably be late getting back on the water, and lose a lot of sailing enjoyment. If the boat is to remain in the water all season long, it will be necessary to coat the bottom with antifouling paint. There are several different types of antifouling paint, as well as different formulas for salt and fresh water. The best procedure is to inquire about the most effective type of paint for your area. As you will discover, some paints seem to perform better than others. Of course, if you plan to trailer your boat, antifouling paint is not necessary, for the boat will probably not be in the water long enough for any bottom growth to develop. There isn't room here to discuss other painting tasks you may face. The hull or topside of the boat, for example, may require painting after several seasons of service. If this is the case, it would be

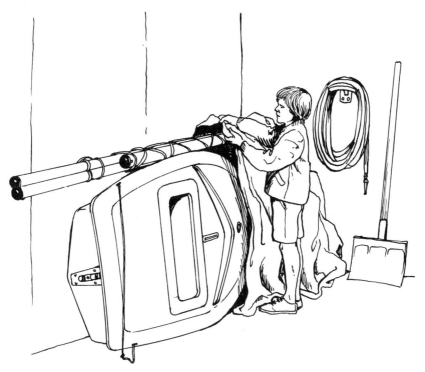

A sailboard is easy to store during the off season. One way is to stand the boat on its side in the garage and cover it with a cloth. Another is to suspend the boat from the garage rafters.

wise to consult a local marine-paint dealer for the best paint available.

Another necessary spring chore is varnishing the *brightwork*. You will discover that much of the varnished woodwork on the boat will need a new coat or two every year. Sand the old coat down with fine sandpaper before applying the new coat. If the old varnish is checked or otherwise broken, consult the instructions on the varnish can for preparing the surface.

Another important spring chore is a complete inspection of all fittings and rigging. Be particularly sure that all fittings that handle line, such as fairleads and cleats, are tight. Tighten those that have loosened. Clean all metal, and polish it to protect against the elements. Make a particularly close inspection of the tiller and rudder assembly. Look for excessive wear, and check to be sure the rudder hasn't warped. Thoroughly clean the interior of the cockpit and cuddy, and return all loose gear that you removed at fall lay-up time. Finally, run through a checklist of required and extra safety gear, and repair or replace wherever necessary.

If your boat has aluminum spars, it will be necessary to clean them with an abrasive substance and then apply polish or wax. Aluminum oxidizes, and over the winter it will collect a layer of oxide scale. Anodized aluminum, on the other hand, does not need to be scrubbed down with an abrasive. It only requires a good washing before application of a protective coating of wax. A good-quality automobile wax does a very satisfactory job. A final chore on the mast is inspection of all rigging and fittings. In particular, carefully examine the halyard for wear. If any wear is evident, it is probably a good idea to replace the halyard rather than take a chance on it.

MIDSEASON CARE

Care for your boat does not end once it has been launched. Throughout the sailing season, there are a number of inspection and maintenance chores you should carry out routinely. The running rigging, for example, should be inspected for wear each time you go out sailing. In addition, make periodic checks of all standing rigging. Pay particular attention to wire rigging, especially where the wire passes over pulleys or sheaves.

If you are going to race your boat, its bottom will need periodic cleaning. This is especially true if the boat is left in the water all season long. Even the best anti-fouling paints will not prevent the growth of marine or aquatic slimes. As a result, it will be necessary to haul the

*If you are going to race your sailboard, it will be
necessary to keep it in top condition. Check all fittings
and rigging, and make sure the bottom of the boat is
scrubbed clean before each race. (Photo courtesy of
AMF Alcort)*

boat out for a good scrub every month or six weeks.
Another way to do it is to bring the boat in close to
shore and then go into the water to scrub down the
bottom. This takes a good swimmer, for it is necessary to
take a deep breath and duck under while scrubbing.

Sails also require care. Most sailboard sails are made
of Dacron. This synthetic material should be kept clean
of oil or grease. Use a spot remover such as carbon tet-
rachloride to remove any oil or grease spots, but be sure
to work in a well-ventilated area. In addition, try to
remember to keep extreme heat away from Dacron, and
avoid sharp creases in the material.

If you think of your boat as a structure that requires
maintaining, it becomes easier to attend to the routine
inspections needed to keep the craft in top condition.

Actually, little more than a watchful eye is required, followed up immediately with service or repair, to keep your boat in top condition. But it is necessary to "think maintenance"; a sailboat will go downhill rapidly if it is not cared for. This is part of the fun of sailing, however. A skipper takes pride in his craft; thus he willingly assumes responsibility for its condition.

FALL CARE

Fall means the end of the boating season for most sailors. Of course, those who live in states such as Florida or California can enjoy sailing all year round. These sailors are to be envied by the rest of us who must lay up our boats for the long winter. Preparing a sailboard for winter storage consists of more than just hauling it out and stacking it away under a winter cover. Certain chores must be performed if the boat is to get through the winter without damage, and if getting it back into the water the following spring is to be accomplished easily.

One important task is to throroughly clean the entire hull. This includes scrubbing away all dirt, grime, and any residue of marine or aquatic growth from the bottom. The deck, cockpit, and cuddy should be washed down also. In addition, wash down any scum or dirt that has accumulated on the daggerboard or rudder and tiller assembly. Examine all woodwork, and if varnishing is needed, mark the calendar so that you will get to this job early in the spring.

All loose gear should be removed from the boat before putting it in storage. Be especially careful to remove items that may be affected by cold weather. Above all, do not leave any food in the cuddy. It will just attract insects and mice, and also confront you with a messy situation when you pull off the winter cover the following spring.

Finally, do not neglect to care for your sail during the off season. Inspect it carefully, and if any repairs are necessary, get it to a nearby sailmaker for mending and washing as soon as possible. Many sailmakers also store sails during the winter. Don't wait until early spring to have your sail repaired. If you take it to a sailmaker during the fitting-out season, you may wait a long time before getting it back. Thus you could miss much of the fine early-season sailing that characterizes many U.S. waters.

Don't be left out when the sailing season starts. If you've taken proper care of your boat at fall lay-up time and during spring fitting out, you'll be ready to go early, as these sailors are. (Photo by Dorothy I. Crossley)

Buying a Sailboard

How does one go about buying a sailboard (or any sailboat, for that matter)? A good question, and by no means a simple task, for there are many boats to choose from and several levels of quality available. The simplest way to find a boat, but perhaps not the best, is to look for what you are after in the classified section of the newspaper. You will no doubt find sailboards advertised, both new and used. How wide the choice will be, however, is quite another matter. Very likely one or two nationally known types will be available, with all others manufactured and sold locally only. You might very well end up with a poorly designed and manufactured boat under these circumstances.

A much better approach involves studying the characteristics of all of the boats available, and then examining and trying out the boats that seem likely choices. A first step is writing the American Sailing Council, National Association of Engine and Boat Manufacturers, 537 Steamboat Road, Greenwich, Connecticut 06830, for advice. A second step is a careful study of the boats listed in one of the nationally distributed annual buyer's guides. Three such publications are:

Boat Owners Buyers Guide, Yachting Publishing Corporation, 50 West 44th Street, New York, New York 10036.

Sailboat and Sailboat Equipment Directory, Institute for Advancement of Sailing, Inc., 38 Commercial Wharf, Boston, Massachusetts 02110.

Sailboats, One-Design Yachtsman, Inc., P. O. Box 222, Rowayton, Connecticut 06853.

Finally, having established the type, size, and price range suitable to your needs, you should locate the appropriate dealers and examine and try out the sailboards that interest you. Do not, however, overlook a sailboat show, if one is held near your home. Many, many sailboards are displayed at these shows.

Take your time and be selective when buying, and you will go a long way toward making your purchase a source of great enjoyment for many years to come. Good sailing always!

Glossary

ABAFT: farther aft; "abaft the beam," for example, is aft of the beam.

ABEAM: off the side of a boat at an angle of ninety degrees to the centerline.

AFT: in the direction of the stern.

AHEAD: in the direction of the vessel's bow.

ALEE: away from the direction of the wind.

AMIDSHIPS: at the center of a vessel, in terms of either length or width.

ANCHOR: an iron or steel device designed to hold a vessel when dropped to the bottom.

ANCHORAGE: a suitable place for dropping anchor.

ANTICYCLONE: a wind system rotating clockwise around a region of high atmospheric pressure.

APPARENT WIND: wind direction as given by a tell-tale or pennant on a moving boat; apparent wind is slightly forward of the true wind direction.

ASTERN: in the direction of the vessel's stern.

BACKWIND: a wind that strikes the leeward (away from the wind) side of a sail after it has passed over another sail.

BAROMETER: an instrument that measures atmospheric pressure.

BATTENS: thin, rigid strips that fit into pockets along the after edge of a sail; battens help to hold the shape of a sail.

BEAM: the greatest width of a vessel, usually amidships.

BEAM REACH: sailing position with the wind approximately at right angles to the course of the boat.

BEAM WIND: a wind blowing at right angles to the fore-and-aft centerline of a vessel.

BEAT: to sail to windward by alternate tacks.

BEFORE THE WIND: sailing with the wind astern—that is, with the wind coming from directly behind the vessel; see *running*.

BEND: to fasten a sail to the boom and mast; also to fasten one rope to another.

BILGE: the portion of the inside hull below the floorboards.

BOOM: spar at the bottom of a sail.

BOOM VANG: a rig attached to the boom to hold it down and thus to flatten the sail.

BOW: the forward part of the hull of a vessel.

BOW CHOCKS: metal fittings situated on either side of the bow that lead anchor or mooring lines inboard.

BRIDLE: a span of rope to which the sheet line is attached.

BRIGHTWORK: varnished woodwork and polished brass aboard a vessel.

BRISTOL FASHION: in a seamanlike manner.

BROACH: to swing around toward the wind when running free, thus placing the vessel broadside to wind and waves.

BROAD REACH: sailing position between beam reaching and running before the wind, with the wind coming from off the quarter.

BUOY: a floating marker used for piloting; see *can buoy* and *nun buoy*.

BURDENED VESSEL: a vessel required by law to stay clear of another vessel holding the right of way.

BY THE LEE: running with the wind on the same side as the boom.

CAN BUOY: a black cylindrical buoy carrying an odd number that marks the left, or port side of a channel when a vessel is approaching from seaward.

CAPSIZE: to overturn.

CHAIN PLATES: metal straps bolted to the side of a vessel that secure the shrouds.

CHINE: intersection of a hull's side and bottom.

CHOCK: a metal fitting that leads lines over the side of a vessel.

CLEAT: a horn-shaped fitting used to secure a line.

CLEW: the aftermost corner of a fore-and-aft-rigged sail.

CLOSEHAULED: sailing as close to the direction of the wind as efficiency permits.

CLOSE REACH: a sailing position between beating and beam reaching, with the wind forward of the beam.

COAMING: raised railing around a cockpit to prevent water from running in.

COCKPIT: opening at center or after end of a sailboat for passengers or feet.

COLD FRONT: the advancing edge of a cold air mass.

COME UP INTO THE WIND: steer the vessel toward the eye of the wind; see *head up* and *luff up*.

COMING ABOUT: going from one tack to the other by passing the bow through the eye of the wind.

COURSE: the heading of a vessel as measured by the compass.

CRINGLE: ring sewn into a sail through which a line can be passed.

CUDDY: a small shelter cabin or storage locker on many sailboats.

CURRENT: a horizontal movement of water caused by tide, wind, or gravity.

CYCLONE: a wind system rotating counterclockwise around a region of low atmospheric pressure.

DAGGERBOARD: a type of centerboard not hinged, but rather raised and lowered vertically in a well or trunk.

DAGGERBOARD WELL: opening through the hull of a sailboat to accommodate the daggerboard.

DANGER ZONE: region looking forward from a motorboat ranging from dead ahead to two points abaft the starboard beam; a motorboat having another vessel in its danger zone must stay clear.

DISPLACEMENT: the weight of water displaced by a vessel, thus the vessel's own weight.

DISPLACEMENT HULL: a heavy hull with a deep keel that pushes the water aside when under way.

DOUSE: to lower or drop suddenly, as in "douse the sails."

DRAFT: the "belly" or fullness of a sail; also the depth of water needed to float a vessel.

EBB TIDE: the tide during its passage from high to low water.

EVEN KEEL: floating level, not heeled over or listing.

EYE OF THE WIND: the exact direction from which the wind is coming.

FLOOD TIDE: the tide during its passage from low to high water.

FLOORBOARDS: planking on the bottom of the cockpit.

FLOTSAM: floating debris.

FOGBOUND: held in port or at anchor because of fog.

FOOT WELL: small depression in the deck of a sailboat to accommodate the feet of the crew.

FORE-AND-AFT: in line or parallel with the keel.

FORE-AND-AFT RIG: sails mounted parallel with the keel.

FORWARD: in front of, as in "forward of the beam."

FOUL: snarl or tangle; the opposite of clear.

FOUND: furnished; a vessel is said to be "well found" if it is well equipped.

FREEBOARD: the distance from the top of the hull to the water.

FROM THE QUARTER: a direction; wind from the quarter is wind coming in to the boat from 135 to 180 degrees from its heading.

GAFF: the spar that supports the head of a lateen sail.

GENOA: a large jib whose area overlaps the mainsail.

GHOSTING: making headway when there is no apparent wind.

GOOSENECK: the fitting that fastens the boom to the mast.

GUDGEON: an eye fitting on the transom into which the rudder's *pintle* is inserted.

GUNWALE: the rail of a vessel at deck level.

HALYARDS: lines used to hoist the sails.

HARD-A-LEE: the final command in the coming-about sequence; it is given just before putting the tiller over hard to the side opposite the wind.

HAUL: to pull on a line; also said of wind that has shifted toward the bow.

HEADSAILS: all sails set forward of the foremast (the single mast on a sloop).

HEADSTAY: a wire-rope mast support running from the top or near the top of the mast to the bow.

HEAD UP: to point the bow of the vessel more nearly into the wind; see *luff up.*

HEADWAY: motion ahead.

HEEL: to tip or list to one side.

HELM: the tiller or wheel.

HIGH: a region of high atmospheric pressure, as opposed to a *low.*

HIKE OUT: to climb to windward on a sailboat to prevent excessive heeling to leeward.

HULL: the body of a vessel, not including spars and gear.

IN IRONS: when a sailboat is head to wind with the sails luffing, and the bow not paying off on either tack; also called *in stays*.

INSHORE: toward the shore.

JETTISON: to throw overboard.

JIB: a triangular sail set forward of the foremast (the single mast on a sloop).

JIBE: to change a sailboat's course from one tack to the other with the wind aft.

JIBSHEET: the line from the lower aft end of the jib to the cockpit; used to control the set of the jib.

JURY RIG: any makeshift rig.

KEEL: the fore-and-aft timber along the centerline of a vessel; on keel sailboats, the keel extends well below the rest of the hull and provides weight stability and lateral resistance.

KNOCKABOUT: the correct (although rarely used) term for a sloop without a bowsprit.

KNOCKDOWN: when a vessel is thrown on its beam ends by a sudden gust of wind.

KNOT: a measure of speed meaning *nautical miles per hour* (one nautical mile equals 6,080.20 feet); also a method of binding objects together using rope.

LAND BREEZE: an evening breeze blowing from land to sea.

LATEEN RIG: a triangular sail with the boom and gaff meeting at the forward point of the triangle.

LEEWARD: away from the direction of the wind.

LEEWAY: the distance a sailboat is carried to leeward by the force of the wind.

LINES: ropes on a vessel that are used for special purposes, such as *sheet lines, bow lines, or guy lines.*

LOOSE-FOOTED: a sail fastened to a boom at tack and clew only, or without a boom.

LOW: a region of low atmospheric pressure, as opposed to a *high.*

LUFF: the forward edge of a sail; also the fluttering of a sail as it begins to be backwinded.

LUFF UP: to steer more closely into the wind; see *head up.*

MAINSAIL: fore-and-aft sail set on the afterside of the mainmast.

MAINSHEET: the line from the main boom to the cockpit; used to control the set of the mainsail.

MARCONI CAT RIG: a rig in which the Marconi sail is mounted on a mast set well forward, and there are no headsails.

MARCONI SAIL: a tall jib-headed triangular sail.

MAST: a vertical spar that supports spars, rigging, and sails.

MASTHEAD: the top of the mast; a rig in which the headsails extend to the top of the mast.

MOORING: a large permanent anchor and buoy; generally a vessel's permanent home.

NAUTICAL MILE: a unit of distance equal to 6,080.20 feet; see *knot.*

NEAP TIDES: tides of minimum range occurring at the first and third quarters of the moon.

OCCLUDED FRONT: front formed when a cold air mass overtakes a warm air mass and lifts the warm air above the surface of the earth.

OFFSHORE: away from the shore.

OFF THE WIND: sailing on any course except to windward.

ON THE BEAM: a point ninety degrees away from the direction of the course of the boat.

ON THE QUARTER: a direction from 135 to 180 degrees from the heading of the boat.

ON THE WIND: sailing to windward; see *beat* and *closehauled*.

OUTBOARD: beyond the side of a vessel.

OUTHAUL: a line used to fasten and tighten the clew of a sail.

PAINTER: a short length of rope attached to the bow of a small boat.

PAY OFF: to swing away from the wind.

PAY OUT: to ease or feed out a rope or line.

PENNANT: a small narrow flag; also the length of rope that attaches a vessel to its mooring float.

PFD: "personal flotation device"—the new U. S. Coast Guard term for "life preserver."

PINCHING: sailing too close to the wind.

PINTLE: a pinlike metal fitting on the rudder that inserts into the *gudgeon*, which is attached to the boat's transom.

PLANING: a type of sailing in which the hull skims along the surface of the water; some sailboards are capable of planing.

PLANING HULL: a very nearly flat-bottomed hull capable of planing.

POINT: the ability to sail to windward; a sailboat that "points well" sails close to the wind.

PORT: the left side of a vessel facing forward.

PORT TACK: sailing with the wind coming in to the boat over the port side.

PRAM: a small dinghy having square ends.

PRIVILEGED VESSEL: the vessel holding the right of way; the *burdened vessel* must keep clear.

QUARTER: that portion of a vessel forward of the stern and aft of the beam.

QUARTERING SEA: a sea running toward either the port or starboard quarter of a vessel.

RAIL: the outer edge of the deck on a vessel.

RAKE: the angle of a mast from the vertical.

REACH: a sailing course between running free and close-hauled.

READY ABOUT: the initial order given when it is desired to bring a sailboat about.

REEF: a technique for reducing sail area.

RIG: the nature of a sailboat's mast and sail arrangement, as in cat rig, jib-headed rig, and lateen rig.

RIGGING: a term applying to all lines, stays, and shrouds on a sailboat.

RIGHT: to return a vessel to its normal position, as in "righting a capsized boat."

RIGHT OF WAY: the right of the privileged vessel to hold course and speed.

RODE: the anchor line or cable.

RUDDER: the flat plate hinged at or near the stern that is used to steer a vessel; the rudder is controlled by the *tiller*.

RULES OF THE ROAD: the laws of navigation; their primary purpose is the avoidance of collisions.

RUNNING: sailing on a course with the wind astern or on the quarter; see *before the wind*.

RUNNING RIGGING: the movable part of a sailboat's rigging; for example, the halyards and sheet lines.

SEA BREEZE: an afternoon breeze blowing from sea to land.

SEAWAY: an area of sea with moderate or heavy seas running.

SEAWORTHY: capable of putting to sea and meeting sea conditions.

SHEET LINE: a line that controls the set of the sails; see *jibsheet* and *mainsheet.*

SHIPSHAPE: neat and seamanlike.

SHOOT UP INTO THE WIND: to steer the sailboat's bow into the eye of the wind under the boat's momentum.

SHOVE OFF: to depart.

SHROUDS: the rigging that supports a mast at its sides.

SLACK: to ease off; also loose or unfastened; also the state of the tide when there is no horizontal water motion.

SLOOP: a one-masted sailboat, carrying mainsail and jib.

SNUB: to check or stop a rope suddenly.

SPAR: term applied to masts, booms, gaffs, etc.

SPINNAKER: a light balloonlike sail used when running and reaching.

SPLASHBOARD: a raised board on deck designed to deflect spray away from the cockpit.

SPLICE: a method for weaving strands of rope together.

SPRING TIDES: tides of greater-than-average range occurring at new and full moon.

SQUALL: a sudden and violent local storm or gust of wind.

STANDING RIGGING: the part of a sailboat's rigging—
that is, the *shrouds* and *stays*—that support the mast.

STARBOARD: the right side of a vessel facing forward.

STARBOARD TACK: sailing with the wind coming in
to the boat over the starboard side.

STATIONARY FRONT: the boundary line between a
cold air mass and a warm air mass when neither is
replacing the other.

STAYS: the rigging running forward and aft that supports the mast; see *headstay*.

STEERAGE WAY: sufficient headway for the rudder to
function.

STERN: the after end of a vessel.

STOW: to store away on a vessel.

SWAMP: to sink by filling with water.

TACK: to come about; also the lower forward corner of
a sail; also a course sailed, such as the *port tack* and
the *starboard tack*.

TACKLE: a combination of blocks and rope—a "block
and tackle."

TAUT: having no slack.

TELLTALE: a strip of ribbon or yarn tied to a shroud
to show the direction of the apparent wind.

TENDER: lacking stability; also a small boat used for
ferrying passengers.

THWARTSHIPS: at right angles to the fore-and-aft line
on a vessel; from side to side.

TIDAL CURRENT: horizontal flow of water caused by
tidal changes.

TIDE: the rise and fall of the sea level.

TIDE RIPS: areas of disturbed and turbulent water
caused by strong tidal currents.

TILLER: a rod used to control the rudder.

TO LEEWARD: away from the direction of the wind.

TO WINDWARD: into the wind.

TOPSIDE: on deck.

TOPSIDES: the sides of a vessel between the waterline and the rail.

TRANSOM: the stern planking of a square-sterned vessel.

TRAVELER: a metal rod that allows a sheet block to slide back and forth; if rope is used instead, it becomes a *bridle*.

TRIM: the fore-and-aft balance of a vessel; also to adjust the sails to take best advantage of the wind.

UNDER WAY: in motion and under control of the helmsman.

UP ANCHOR: the command to raise the anchor and get under way.

VANG: see *boom vang*.

VEER: when the wind changes direction toward the stern.

WAKE: the track a vessel leaves astern as it passes through the water.

WARM FRONT: the advancing edge of a warm air mass.

WATERLINE: a line painted on a vessel's side to indicate its proper trim.

WEATHER SIDE: the windward side.

WELL FOUND: a well-equipped vessel with all gear in good condition.

WHISKER POLE: a spar used to hold the clew of the jib away from the boat when running before the wind.

WIND AFT: wind coming from directly behind the boat.

WIND AHEAD: wind coming from within forty-five degrees of the heading of the boat.

WINDWARD: toward the wind; the weather side of a vessel.

WING-AND-WING: running before the wind with the main and jib set on opposite sides of the boat.

YACHT: any vessel designed for pleasure use.

Index

ABOUT THE AUTHOR

At the age of thirteen, Lee Drummond built his own fourteen-foot skiff, and he has been sailing now for over twenty-five years. He has taught sailing as well as swimming, life saving, canoeing, and boating, and has racing experience in the Lightning Class and in cruising yachts. He was born in New York City, received his B.A. degree from Bowdoin College, and graduate degrees from Hofstra and Wesleyan universities. Mr. Drummond, who has also written *The Complete Beginner's Guide to Sailing* and *The Complete Beginner's Guide to Outboarding*, is editor-in-chief of the school science department for a major textbook publishing company. He lives in Bedford, Massachusetts, with his wife, who is also an avid sailor.